THE CONSCIOUSNESS OF THE ATOM

THE CONSCIOUSNESS OF THE ATOM

by

ALICE A. BAILEY

A series of lectures delivered in New York City
Winter of 1921-22.

Author of

"Letters on Occult Meditation"
"Initiation, Human and Solar"

KALPAZ

ISBN: 978-93-5128-945-6(HB)

First Published in 1922
Indian Reprint in 2017

Published by

Kalpaz Publications
C-30, Satyawati Nagar,
Delhi – 110052
E-mail: kalpaz@hotmail.com
Website: kalpazpublications.com
Ph.: +91-9212142040

TABLE OF CONTENTS.

LECTURE I.

The Field of Evolution. 1

LECTURE II.

The Evolution of Substance. 15

LECTURE III.

The Evolution of Form, or Group Evolution. 31

LECTURE IV.

The Evolution of Man, the Thinker. 47

LECTURE V.

The Evolution of Consciousness. 60

LECTURE VI.

The Goal of Evolution. 75

LECTURE VII.

Cosmic Evolution. 93

FOREWORD

The lectures here presented were delivered in New York during the past winter. The purpose of this series was to present to their auditors the testimony of science as to the relation of matter and of consciousness; to enable the hearers to observe the identical manifestation of these relations and of certain basic laws in successively higher states of being, and thus to bring to them a realization of the universality of the evolutionary process and its actuality; and to deal somewhat with the nature of the expanded states of consciousness and the enlarged life toward which all mankind is traveling. They thus were intended to serve as an introduction to the more detailed study and application of the laws of life and human unfoldment generally included in the term of "occultism."

It will be observed that there is in this series a considerable amount of repetition, as each lecture briefly reviews the matters covered in the preceding addresses. As newcomers were present at each lecture in the series, it was found necessary on each occasion to present a bird's eye view of the ground covered and the reasons for the position then taken. A further advantage was found in the fixing in the minds of the hearers of certain of these basic concepts which were new to many of them, and which helped to enable them to grasp and to receive readily the further expansion of the theme. In presenting the lectures in book form it has been deemed advisable to retain the complete text of the lectures as given. Those who are already students of the esoteric wisdom will be able to follow the line of the argument of the lectures without difficulty. For those however, who for the first time approach the consideration of the matters here discussed, the occasional repetition of the fundamental points may help to a ready apprehension, and it is for this class of readers that the book is primarily intended.

ALICE A. BAILEY

September, 1922.

THE CONSCIOUSNESS OF THE ATOM.

LECTURE I.

THE FIELD OF EVOLUTION.

There has probably never been a period in the history of thought entirely resembling the present. Thinkers everywhere are conscious of two things, first, that the region of mystery has never before been so clearly defined, and secondly, that that region can be entered more easily than has hitherto been the case; it may, therefore, perhaps be induced to render up some of its secrets if investigators of all schools pursue their search with determination. The problems with which we are faced, as we study the known facts of life and existence, are susceptible of clearer definition than heretofore, and though we do not know the answer to our questions, though we have not as yet discovered the solution to our problems, though no panacea lies ready to our hand whereby we can remedy the world's ills, yet the very fact that we can define them, that we can point in the direction in which mystery lies, and that the light of science, of religion, and of philosophy, has been shed upon vast tracts which were earlier considered lands of darkness, is a guarantee of success in the future. We know so much more than was the case five hundred years ago, except in a few circles of wise men and mystics; we have discovered so many laws of nature, even though as yet we cannot apply them, and the knowledge of "things as they are" (and I choose these words very deliberately) has made immense strides.

Nevertheless, the mystery land still remains to be opened up, and our problems are still numerous. There is the problem of our own particular life, whatever that may be; there is the problem of that which is largely termed the "Not-Self", and which concerns our physical body, our environment, our circumstances, and our life conditions; if we are of an introspective turn of mind, there is the problem of our particular set of emotions, and of the thoughts, desires, and instincts by which we control action. Group problems are many; why should there be suffering, starvation, and pain? Why should the world as a whole be in the thrall of the direst poverty, of sickness, of discomfort? What is the purpose underlying all that we see around us, and what will be the outcome of world affairs, viewing them as a whole? What is the destiny of the human race, what is its origin, and what is the key to its present condition? Is there more than this one life, and is the sole interest to be found in that which is apparent and material? Such queries pass through all our minds at various times, and have passed through the minds of thinkers right down through the centuries.

There have been many attempts to reply to these questions, and as we study them, we find that the answers given fall into three main groups, and that three principal solutions are held out for the consideration of men. These three solutions are:—

First, *Realism.* Another name for this school is that of Materialism. It teaches that "the presentation which we have in consciousness of an external world is true"; that things are what they seem; that matter and force, as we know them, are the only reality, and that it is not possible for man to get beyond the tangible. He should be satisfied with facts as he knows them, or as science tells him they are. This is a perfectly legitimate method of solution, but for some of us it fails in that it does not go far enough. In refusing to concern itself with anything except that which can be proven and demonstrated it stops short at the very point where the enquirer says, "that is so, but why?" It leaves out of its calculation much that is known and realised as truth by the average man, even though he may be unable to explain why he knows it to be true. Men everywhere are recognising the accuracy of the facts of the realistic school, and of material science, yet at the same time they feel innately that there is, underlying the proven objective manifestation, some vitalising force, and some coherent purpose which cannot be accounted for in terms of matter alone.

Secondly, there is the point of view which we can best, perhaps, call *supernaturalism*. Man becomes conscious that perhaps, after all, things are not exactly what they seem to be, and that there remains much which is inexplicable; he awakens to the realisation that he himself is not simply an accumulation of physical atoms, a material something, and a tangible body, but that latent within him is a consciousness, a power, and a psychic nature which link him to all other members of the human family, and to a power outside himself which he must perforce explain. This it is which has led, for instance, to the evolution of the Christian and Jewish point of view, which posits a God outside the solar system, Who created it, but was Himself extraneous to it. These systems of thought teach that the world has been evolved by a Power or Being Who has built the solar system, and Who guides the worlds aright, keeping our little human life in the hollow of His hand, and "sweetly ordering" all things according to some hidden purpose which it is not possible for us, with our finite minds, to glimpse, still less to understand. This is the religious and supernatural point of view, and is based on the growing selfconsciousness of the individual, and in a recognition of his own divinity. Like the point of view of the realistic school, it embodies only a partial truth, and needs to be complemented.

The third line of thought we might call the *Idealistic.* It posits an evolutionary process within all manifestation, and identifies life with the cosmic process. It is the exact opposite of materialism, and brings the supernatural deity, predicated by the religionist, into the position of a great Entity or Life, Who is evolving through, and by means of, the universe, just as man is evolving consciousness through the medium of an objective physical body.

In these three standpoints—the frankly materialistic, the purely supernatural, and the idealistic—you have the three main lines of thought which have been put forward as explanatory of the cosmic process; all of them are partial truths, yet none of them is complete without the others, all of them, when followed alone, lead into byways and into darkness, and leave the central mystery still unsolved. When synthesised, when brought together and blended, and when unified, they embody, perhaps, (I offer this simply as a suggestion) just as much of the evolutionary truth as it is possible for the human mind to grasp at the present stage of evolution.

We are dealing with large problems, and tampering, perhaps, with high and lofty things; we are trespassing into regions which are the recognised domain of metaphysics; and we are endeavouring to sum up in a few brief talks what all the libraries of the world are embodying; we are therefore attempting the impossible. All that we can do is to take up briefly and cursorily first one aspect of the truth and then another. All we can possibly accomplish is an outline of the basic lines of evolution, a study of their relationship to each other and to ourselves as conscious entities, and then an endeavour to blend and synthesise the little we can know until some general idea of the process as a whole becomes clearer.

We have to remember in connection with every statement of truth that each is made from a particular point of view. Until we have further developed our mental processes, and until we are able to think in abstract terms as well as in concrete, it will not be possible for us to fully answer the question, What is truth? nor to express any aspect of that truth in a perfectly unbiassed way. Some people have a wider horizon than others, and some can see the unity underlying the differing aspects. Others are prone to think that their outlook and interpretation is the only one. I hope in these talks to broaden somewhat our point of view. I hope we shall come to the realisation that the man who is only interested in the scientific aspect, and who confines himself to the study of those manifestations which are purely material, is just as much occupied with the study of the divine as is his frankly religious brother who only concerns himself with the spiritual side; and that the philosopher is, after all, occupied in emphasising for us the very necessary aspect of the intelligence which links the matter aspect and the spiritual, and blends them into one coherent whole. Perhaps by the union of these three lines of science, religion, and philosophy, we may get a working knowledge of the truth as it is, remembering at the same time that "truth lies within ourselves." No one man's expression of the truth is the whole expression, and the sole purpose of thought is to enable us to build constructively for ourselves, and to work in mental matter.

I should like to outline my plan this evening, to lay the groundwork for our future talks, and to touch upon the main lines of evolution. The line that is most apparent is necessarily that which deals with the evolution of *substance,* with the study of the atom, and the nature of atomic matter. Next week we will touch upon that. Science has much to tell us about the evolution of the atom, and has wandered a long way during the past fifty years from the standpoint of the last century. Then the atom was regarded as an indivisible unit of substance; now it is looked upon as a centre of energy, or electric force. From the evolution of substance we are led very naturally to the evolution of forms, or of congeries of atoms, and there will then open up to us the interesting consideration of forms other than the purely material,—forms existing in subtler substance, such as forms of thought, and the racial forms, and the forms of organisations. In this dual study, one of the aspects of deity will be emphasised, should you choose to use the term "deity", or one of the manifestations of nature, should you prefer that less sectarian expression.

We shall then be led to the consideration of the evolution of intelligence, or of the factor of mind which is working out as ordered purpose in all that we see around us. This will reveal to us a world which is not blindly going on its way, but which has back of it some plan, some coordinated scheme, some organised concept which is working itself out by means of the material form. One reason why things appear to us so difficult of comprehension is involved in the fact that we are in the midst of a transition period, and the plan is as yet imperfect; we are too close to the machinery, being ourselves an integral part of the whole. We see a little bit of it here, and another little bit there, but the whole grandeur of the idea is not apparent to us. We may have a vision, we may have a high moment of revelation, but when we contact the reality on every side, we question the possibility of the ideal materialising, for the intelligent relationship between the form and that which utilises it seems so far from adjustment.

The recognition of the factor of the intelligence will inevitably lead us to the contemplation of the evolution of consciousness in its many forms, ranging all the way from those types of consciousness which we consider sub-human, through the human, up to what may be logically posited (even if it may not be demonstrated) to be super-human consciousness. The next question which will face us will be, what lies back of all these factors? Is there, behind the objective form and its animating intelligence, an evolution which corresponds to the "I" faculty, to the Ego in man? Is there in nature, and in all that we see around us, the working out of the purpose of an individualised selfconscious Being? If there is such a Being, and such a fundamental existence, we should be able to see somewhat His intelligent activities, and to watch His plans working towards fruition. Even if we cannot prove that God is, and that the Deity exists, it may be possible to say, at least, that the hypothesis that He exists is a reasonable one, a rational suggestion, and a possible solution of all the mysteries we see around us. But to do that it has to be demonstrated that there is an intelligent purpose working through forms of every kind, through races and nations, and through all that we see manifesting in modern civilisation; the steps that that purpose has taken, and the gradual growth of the plan, will have to be demonstrated, and from that demonstration we shall perhaps be able to see what lies ahead for us in the coming stages.

Let us for a minute consider what we mean by the words "evolutionary process". They are constantly being used, and the average man well knows that the word "evolution" suggests an unfolding from within outwards, and the unrolling from an inner centre, but we need to define the idea more clearly, and thus get a better concept. One of the best definitions which I have come across is that which defines evolution as "the unfolding of a continually increasing power to respond." Here we have a definition that is very illuminating as we consider the matter aspect of manifestation. It involves the conception of vibration, and of response to vibration, and though we may in time have to discard the term "matter", and employ some such expression as "force centre", the concept still holds good, and the response of the centre to stimulation is even more accurately to be seen. In considering human consciousness this same definition is of real value. It involves the idea of a gradually increasing realisation, of the developing response of the subjective life to its environment, and it leads us eventually on and up to the ideal of a unified Existence which will be the synthesis of all the lines of evolution, and to a conception of a central Life, or force, which blends and holds together all the evolving units, whether they are units of matter, such as the atom of the chemist and the physicist, or units of consciousness, such as human beings. This is evolution, the process which unfolds the life within all units, the developing urge which eventually merges all units and all groups, until you have that sum total of manifestation which can be called Nature, or God, and which is the aggregate of all the states of consciousness. This is the God to Whom the Christian refers when he says "in Him we live, and move, and have our being"; this is the force, or energy, which the scientist recognises; and this is the universal mind, or the Oversoul of the philosopher. This, again, is the intelligent Will which controls, formulates, binds, constructs, develops, and brings all to an ultimate perfection. This is that Perfection which is inherent in matter itself, and the tendency which is latent in the atom, in man, and in all that is. This interpretation of the evolutionary process does not look upon it as the result of an outside Deity pouring His energy and wisdom upon a waiting world, but rather as something which is latent within that world itself, that lies hidden at the heart of the atom of chemistry, within the heart of man himself, within the planet, and within the solar system. It is that something which drives all on toward the goal, and is the force which is gradually bringing order out of chaos; ultimate perfection out of temporary imperfection; good out of seeming evil; and out of darkness and disaster that which we shall some day recognise as beautiful, right, and true. It is all that we have visioned and conceived of in our highest and best moments.

Evolution has also been defined as "cyclic development", and this definition brings me to a thought which I am very anxious that we should thoroughly grasp. Nature repeats continuously until certain definite ends have been reached, certain concrete results have been brought about, and certain responses made to vibration. It is by the recognition of this accomplishment that the intelligent purpose of indwelling Existence can be demonstrated. The method whereby this is achieved is that of discrimination, or of intelligent choice. There are, in the text-books of different schools, many words which are used to convey the same general idea, such as "natural selection", or "attraction and repulsion". I would like, if possible, to avoid technical terms, because they are used by one school of thought to mean one thing, and by another, something different. If we can find a word similar in intent, yet not tied to any particular line of thought, we may find fresh light thrown upon our problem. Attraction and repulsion in the solar system is but the discriminating faculty of the atom or of man demonstrating in the planets and the sun. It will be found in atoms of all kinds; we can call it adaptation, if we so choose, or the power to grow and to adapt the unit to its environment through the rejection of certain factors and the acceptance of others. It shows itself in man as free will, or the power to choose, and in the spiritual man it can be seen as the tendency to sacrifice, for a man then chooses a particular line of action in order to benefit the group to which he belongs, and rejects that which is purely selfish.

We might finally define evolution as ordered change and constant mutation. It demonstrates in the ceaseless activity of the unit or the atom, the interaction between groups, and the endless play of one force or type of energy upon another.

We have seen that evolution, whether it is of matter, of intelligence, of consciousness, or of spirit, consists in an ever increasing power to respond to vibration, that it progresses through constant change, by the practice of a selective policy or the use of the discriminative faculty, and by the method of psychic development or repetition. The stages which distinguish the evolutionary process might be broadly divided into three, corresponding to the stages in the life of a human being: childhood, adolescence, and maturity. Where man is concerned these stages can be traced in the human unit or in the race, and as the civilisations pass on and increase, it should surely become possible to trace the same threefold idea in the human family as a whole, and thus ascertain the divine objective through the study of His image, or reflection, MAN. We might express these three stages in more scientific terms, and link them with the three schools of thought earlier referred to, studying them as,

a. The stage of atomic energy.
b. The stage of group coherency.
c. The stage of unified or synthetic existence.

Let me see if I can make my meaning clear. The stage of atomic energy is largely that which concerns the material side of life, and corresponds to the childhood period in the life of a man or a race. It is the time of realism, of intense activity, of development by action above all else, or pure self-centredness and self-interest. It produces the materialistic point of view, and leads inevitably to selfishness. It involves the recognition of the atom as being entirely self-contained, and similarly of the human unit as having a separate life apart from all other units, and with no relationship to others. Such a stage can be seen in the little evolved races of the world, in small children, and in those who are little developed. They are normally self-centred; their energies are concerned with their own life; they are occupied with the objective and with that which is tangible; they are characterised by a necessary and protective selfishness. It is a most necessary stage in the development and perpetuation of the race.

Out of this selfish atomic period grows another stage, that of group coherency. This involves the building up of forms or species until you have something coherent and individualised in itself as a whole, yet which is composed of many lesser individualities and forms. In connection with the human being it corresponds to his awakening realisation of responsibility, and to his recognition of his place within the group. It necessitates an ability on his part to recognise a life greater than himself, whether that life is called God, or whether it is simply regarded as the life of the group to which a man, as a unit, belongs, that great Identity of which we are each a part. This corresponds to the school of thought which we called the supernatural, and it must be succeeded in time by a truer and a wider concept. As we have already seen, the first or atomic stage developed by means of selfishness, or the self-centred life of the atom (whether the atom of substance or the human atom); the second stage grows to perfection by the sacrifice of the unit to the good of the many, and of the atom to the group in which it has place. This stage is something which we, as yet, know practically little about, and is what we often vision and hope for.

The third stage lies a long way ahead, and may be considered by many a vain chimera. But some of us have a vision, which, even if unattainable at present, is logically possible if our premises are correct, and our foundation is rightly laid. It is that of unified existence. Not only will there be the separate units of consciousness; not only the differentiated atoms within the form, not only will there be the group made up of a multiplicity of identities, but we shall have the aggregate of all forms, of all groups, and of all states of consciousness blended, unified, and synthesised into a perfected whole. This whole you may call the solar system, you may call it nature, or you may call it God. Names matter not. It corresponds to the adult stage in the human being; it is analogous to the period of maturity, and to that stage wherein a man is supposed to have a definite purpose and life work, and a clear-cut plan in view, which he is working out by the aid of his intelligence. In these talks I should like, if I can, to show that something like this is going on in the solar system, in the planet, in the human family, and in the atom. I trust that we can prove that there is an intelligence underlying all; and that from separation will come union, produced through blending and merging into group formation, and that eventually from the many groups will be seen emerging the one perfect, fully conscious whole, composed of myriads of separated identities animated by one purpose and one will. If this is so, what is the next practical step ahead for those who come to this realisation?

How can we make practical application of this ideal to our own lives, and ascertain our immediate duty so that we may participate in, and consciously further the plan? In the cosmic process we have our tiny share, and each day of activity should see us playing our part with intelligent understanding.

Our first aim should surely be self realisation through the practice of discrimination; we must learn to think clearly for ourselves, to formulate our own thoughts and to manipulate our own mental processes; we must learn to know what we think and why we think it, to find out the nature of our life, and to experiment. We find ourselves, and know ourselves, through the method of discrimination and of selection and rejection.

When this is the practice of our lives, and the habit of our thought, we can then endeavour to find out the meaning of group consciousness through the study of the law of sacrifice. Not only must we find ourselves through the primary childhood stage of selfishness (and surely that should lie behind us), not only should we learn to distinguish between the real and the unreal, through the practice of discrimination, but we should endeavour to pass on from that to something very much better. For us the immediate goal should be to find the group to which we may belong. We do not belong to all groups, nor can we consciously realise our place in the one great Body, but we can find some group in which we have our place, some body of people with whom we can co-operate and work, some brother or brothers whom we can succour and assist. It really involves the conscious contacting of the ideal of brotherhood, and—until we have evolved to the stage where our concept is universal—it means finding the particular set of brothers whom we can love and help by means of the law of sacrifice, and by the transmutation of selfishness into loving service. Thus we can co-operate in the general purpose, and participate in the mission of the group.

Next week we will follow out some of these ideas in connection with the evolution of substance, and the part it plays in the general scheme.

LECTURE II.

THE EVOLUTION OF SUBSTANCE.

It is obvious that in such a series of lectures as this it would be impossible to deal adequately in any way with this stupendous subject, even were I equipped to lecture on such a fundamentally scientific matter. Again, if the conclusions of science were definite upon the evolution of matter, the topic would be, even then, too vast to handle, but they are not, and hence the further complicating of the subject. Therefore I want to preface my remarks tonight by stating that my aim is to speak particularly for those who have no scientific training of any kind, and to give them a general concept of the usually accepted ideas; I seek, then, to make some suggestions which we may find helpful in adjusting our minds to this great problem of matter. Usually when the substance aspect of manifestation has been considered, it has been as a thing apart, and it is only lately that what I might call the "psychology of matter" is beginning to come before the mind of the public through the investigations and conclusions of the broader minded scientists.

You will remember that last week I endeavoured, in a broad and general way, to point out to you that there were three lines of approach to the study of the material universe. There is the line which considers only the materialistic aspect, and is occupied only with that which can be seen, which is tangible, and which can be proven. A second line is that of supernaturalism, which recognises not so much the material side of things as that which is called divine; it deals with the life side, and with the spirit aspect, viewing that Life as a power extraneous to the solar system and to man, and positing that power as a great creative Agent, Who creates and guides the objective universe and yet is outside of it. These two lines of thought can be seen upheld by the frankly materialistic scientist, the orthodox Christian, and the deist of every faith.

I indicated next a third line of approach to the problem, and we called it the idealistic concept. It recognises the material form, but sees also the life within it, and it posits a Consciousness or Intelligence which is evolving by means of that outer form. You will find, I think, that that is the line which I shall emphasise and stress in these lectures. No speaker is able, after all, to dissociate himself entirely from his own point of view, and in these talks I have set myself the task of working along this third line, for to me it synthesises the other two, and adds certain concepts which produce a coherent whole when merged with the other two. It is for you to decide if this third standpoint is logical, reasonable, and clear.

The most common fact in life for all of us is that of the material world,—that world which we can see and contact by means of the five senses, and which is called by the metaphysical thinkers the "not-self", or that which is objective to each one of us. As we all know, the work of the chemist is to reduce all known substances to their very simplest elements, and it was thought not long ago that this had been satisfactorily accomplished. The conclusions of the chemist placed the number of the known elements between seventy and eighty. About twenty years ago, however, (in 1898) a new element was discovered which was called Radium, and this discovery entirely revolutionized the world's thought about matter and substance. If you will go to the text-books of the last century, or search the old dictionaries, seeking for the definition of the atom, for instance, you will usually find Newton quoted. He defined the atom as "a hard, indivisible, ultimate particle", a something which was incapable of further subdivision. This was considered to be the ultimate atom in the universe, and was called by the scientist of the Victorian era "the foundation stone of the universe"; they considered they had gone as far back as it was possible to go, and that they had discovered what lay back of all manifestation and of objectivity itself. But when radium, and the other radio-active substances, had been discovered, an entirely new aspect of the situation had to be faced. It became apparent that what was considered the ultimate particle was not so at all. As you now have the definition of the atom (I am quoting from the Standard Dictionary) it is:

> "An atom is a centre of force, a phase of electrical phenomena, a centre of energy, active through its own internal make-up, and giving off energy or heat or radiation."

Therefore, an atom is (as Lord Kelvin in 1867 thought it would ultimately turn out to be) a "vortex ring", or centre of force, and not a particle of what we understand as tangible substance. This ultimate particle of matter is now demonstrated to be composed of a positive nucleus of energy, surrounded—just as is the sun by the planets—with many electrons or negative corpuscles, thus subdividing the atom of earlier science into numerous lesser bodies. The elements differ according to the number and arrangement of these negative electrons around their positive nucleus, and they rotate or move around this central charge of electricity as our planetary system rotates around the sun. Professor Soddy, in one of his latest books, has pointed out that in the atom is to be seen an entire solar system,—the central sun can be recognised, with the planets pursuing their orbital paths around it.

It would be apparent to each of us that when this definition of the atom is contemplated and studied an entirely new concept of substance comes before us. Dogmatic assertions are therefore out of order, for it is realised that perhaps the next discovery may reveal to us the fact that the electrons themselves may be worlds within worlds. An interesting speculation along these lines is to be found in a book by one of our scientific thinkers in which he suggests that we might be able to divide and subdivide the electron itself into what he calls "psychons", and thus be led into realms which are not now considered physical. That may be only a dream, but the thing that I am seeking to impress upon my mind and yours is that we scarcely know where we stand in scientific thought, any more than we know where we stand in the religious and economic world. Everything is passing through a period of transition; the old order changeth; the old way of looking at things is proving false or inadequate; the old expressions of thought seem futile. All that the wise man can do just now is to reserve his opinion, ascertain for himself what appeals to him as truth, and endeavour then to synthesise that particular aspect of universal truth with that aspect which has been accepted by his brother.

The atom, then, can be predicated as resolving itself into electrons, and can be expressed in terms of force or energy. When you have a centre of energy or activity you are involved in a dual concept; you have that which is the cause of movement or energy, and that which it energises or actuates. This brings us directly into the field of psychology, because energy or force is ever regarded as a quality, and where you have a quality you are really considering the field of psychic phenomena.

There are certain terms in use when considering substance which are continuously appearing, and about which there is a wide diversity of definition. In looking over one scientific book last week it was discouraging to find the author pointing out that the atom of the chemist, of the physicist, of the mathematician, and of the metaphysician were four totally different things. That is another reason why it is not possible to be dogmatic in dealing with these questions. Nevertheless, rightly or wrongly, I have a very definite hypothesis to put before you. When we talk about radium, we are, in all probability, venturing into the realm of etheric substance,. the region of ether, or of protyle. Protyle was a word coined by Sir William Crookes, and is defined by him as follows:

> "Protyle is a word analogous to protoplasm, to express the idea of the original primal matter before the evolution of the chemical elements. The word I have ventured to use for this purpose is compounded of a Greek word 'earlier than', and 'the stuff of which things are made'."

We are, therefore, throwing the concept of matter back to where the oriental school has always put it, to primordial stuff, to that which the orientalist calls "primordial ether", though we must ever remember that the ether of science is many, many removes from the primordial ether of the oriental occultist. We are led back to that intangible something which is the basis of the objective thing which you and I can see and touch and handle. The word "substance" itself means that which "stands under", or which lies back of things. All, therefore, that we can predicate in connection with the ether of space is that it is the medium in which energy or force functions, or makes itself felt.

When we are talking in these lectures of energy and force, and of matter and substance, we can separate them in our minds thus: We speak about energy and substance when we are considering that which is as yet intangible, and we use force in connection with matter when dealing with that aspect of the objective which our scientists are definitely studying. Substance is the ether in one of its many grades, and is that which lies back of matter itself.

When we speak of energy there must be that which energises, that which is the source of energy and the origin of that force which demonstrates in matter. It is here that I seek to lay the emphasis. Whence comes this energy, and what is it?

Scientists are recognising ever more clearly that atoms possess qualities, and it would be interesting if one were to take the different scientific books dealing with the subject of atomic matter, and note which of the many and varying terms applied to them could be applied to a human being also. On a small scale I have attempted this, and found it very illuminating.

First of all, as we know, the atom is spoken of as possessing energy, and the power to change from one mode of activity to another. One writer has remarked that "absolute intelligence thrills through every atom in the world." In this connection I want to point out to you what Edison is reported by an interviewer as having said, in Harper's Magazine for February, 1890, and which is enlarged upon in the Scientific American for October, 1920. In the earlier instance he is quoted as follows:

> "I do not believe that matter is inert, acted upon by an outside force. To me it seems that every atom is possessed by a certain amount of primitive intelligence. Look at the thousands of ways in which atoms of hydrogen combine with those of other elements,

forming the most diverse substances. Do you mean to say that they do this without intelligence? Atoms in harmonious and useful relation assume beautiful or interesting shapes and colours, or give forth a pleasant perfume, as if expressing their satisfaction...... gathered together in certain forms, the atoms constitute animals of the lower order. Finally they combine in man, who represents the total intelligence of all the atoms."

"But where does this intelligence come from originally?" asked the interviewer.

"From some power greater than ourselves," Edison answered.

"Do you believe, then, in an intelligent Creator, a personal God?"

"Certainly. The existence of such a God can, to my mind, be proved from chemistry."

In the long interview quoted last year in the Scientific American, Edison laid down a number of most interesting surmises from which I have culled the following:

1. Life, like matter is indestructible.

2. Our bodies are composed of myriads of infinitesimal entities, each in itself a unit of life; just as the atom is composed of myriads of electrons.

3. The human being acts as an assemblage rather than as a unit; the body and mind express the vote or voice of the life entities.

4. The life entities build according to a plan. If a part of the life organism be mutilated, they rebuild exactly as before......

7. Science admits the difficulty of drawing the line between the inanimate and the animate; perhaps the life entities extend their activities to crystals and chemicals......

9. The life entities live for ever; so that to this extent at least the eternal life which many of us hope for is a reality.

In an address given by Sir Clifford Allbut, President of the British Medical Association, as reported in the Literary Digest of February 26th, 1921, he speaks of the ability of the microbe to select and reject, and in the course of his remarks he says:—

"When the microbe finds itself in the host's body it may be wholly out of tune, or wholly in tune, with any or all cells that it approaches; in either case presumably nothing morbid would happen.........morbid happenings would lie between this microbe and body-cells within its range but not in tune with it. Now there seems to be reason to suppose that a microbe, on its approach to a body cell only just out of its range, may try this way and that to get a hitch on. If so, the microbe, at first innocuous, would become noxious. So, on the other hand, body-cells may educate themselves to vibrate in harmony with a microbe before dissonant: or there may be mutual interchange and co-adaptation......

"But, if things be so, surely we are face to face with a marvelous and far-reaching faculty, the faculty of choice, and this rising from the utter bottom of biology to the summit—formative faculty—'auto-determination', or, if you please, 'mind'."

In the year 1895, Sir William Crookes, one of our greatest scientists, gave an interesting lecture before a body of chemists in Great Britain, in which he dealt with the ability of the atom to choose its own path, to reject and to select, and showed that natural selection can be traced in all forms of life, from the then ultimate atom up through all forms of being.

In another scientific article, the atom is further accused of having sensation as well:

> "The recent contest as to the nature of atoms, which we must regard as in some form or other the ultimate factors in all physical and chemical processes, seems to be capable of easiest solution by the conception that these very minute masses possess—as centres of force—a persistent soul, that every atom has sensation and power of movement."

Tyndall has likewise pointed out that even the very atoms themselves seem to be "instinct with the desire for life."

If you take these different qualities of the atom—energy, intelligence, ability to select and reject, to attract and repulse, sensation, movement, and desire—you have something which is very much like the psychology of a human being, only within a more limited radius and of a more circumscribed degree. Have we not, therefore, really got back to what might be termed the "psyche of the atom"? We have found that the atom is a living entity, a little vibrant world, and that within its sphere of influence other little lives are to be found, and this very much in the same sense as each of us is an entity, or positive nucleus of force or life, holding within our sphere of influence other lesser lives, i.e., the cells of our body. What can be said of us can be said, in degree, of the atom.

Let us extend our idea of the atom a little further, and touch upon what may be fundamentally the cause, and hold the solution of the world problems. This concept of the atom as a positive demonstration of energy, holding within its range of activity its polar opposite, can be extended not only to every type of atom, but also to a human being. We can view each unit of the human family as a human atom, for in man you have simply a larger atom.

He is a centre of positive force, holding within the periphery of his sphere of influence the cells of his body; he shows discrimination, intelligence, and energy. The difference lies but in degree. He is possessed of a wider consciousness, and vibrates to a larger measure than the little atom of the chemist.

We might extend the idea still further and consider a planet as an atom. Perhaps there is a life within the planet that holds the substance of the sphere and all forms of life upon it to itself as a coherent whole, and that has a specific extent of influence. This may sound like a wild speculation, yet, judging from analogy, there may perhaps be within the planetary sphere an Entity Whose consciousness is as far removed from that of man as the consciousness of man is from that of the atom of chemistry.

This thought can again be carried still further, till it includes the atom of the solar system. There, at the heart of the solar system, the sun, you have the positive centre of energy, holding the planets within its sphere of influence. If you have within the atom, intelligence; if you have within the human being, intelligence; if you have within the planet, an Intelligence controlling all its functions, may it not be logical to extend the idea and predicate a still greater Intelligence back of that larger atom, the solar system?

This brings us ultimately to the standpoint which the religious world has always held, that of there being a God, or Divine Being. Where the orthodox Christian would say with reverence, God, the scientist, with equal reverence, would say, Energy; yet they would both mean the same. Where the idealistic teacher would speak of the "God within" the human form, others with equal accuracy would speak of the "energising faculty" of man, which drives him into activity of a physical, emotional, or mental nature.

Everywhere are to be found centres of force, and the idea can be extended from such a force centre as a chemical atom, on and up through varying grades and groups of such intelligent centres, to man, and thence to the Life which is manifesting through the system. Thus is demonstrated a marvellous and synthesised Whole. St. Paul may have had something of this sort in mind when he spoke about the Heavenly Man. By the "body of Christ" he surely means all those units of the human family who are held within His sphere of influence, and who go to the constitution of His body, as the aggregate of the physical cells form the physical body of the man. What is needed in these days of religious upheaval is that these fundamental truths of Christianity should be demonstrated to be scientific truths. We need to make religion scientific.

There is a very interesting Sanskrit writing, many thousands of years old, which I am venturing to quote here. It says:

> "Every form on earth, and every speck (atom) in space, strives in its efforts towards self-formation, and to follow the model placed for it in the Heavenly Man. The involution and the evolution of the atom...... have all one and the same object: man."

Do you note what a large hope this concept opens out before us? Not one atom of matter, showing latent intelligence, discrimination, and selective power, but will, in the course of aeons, reach that more advanced stage of consciousness which we call human. Surely, then, the human atom may equally be supposed to progress to something still more widely conscious, and eventually reach the stage of development of those great Entities whose bodies are planetary atoms; and for Them, as well, what is there? Attainment of that all-including state of consciousness which we call God, or the solar Logos. Surely this teaching is logical and practical. The old occult injunction which said to a man "Know thyself, for in thyself is to be found all that there is to be known," is still the rule for the wise student. If each one of us would scientifically regard ourselves as centres of force, holding the matter of our bodies within our radius of control, and thus working through and in them, we should have a hypothesis whereby the entire cosmic scheme could be interpreted. If, as Einstein hints, our entire solar system is but a sphere, colouring is given to the deduction that it, in its turn, may be but a cosmic atom: thus we would have a place within a still larger scheme, and have a centre around which our system rotates, and in which it is as the electron to the atom. We have been told by astronomers that our entire system is probably revolving around a central point in the heavens.

Thus the basic idea which I have sought to emphasize can be traced all the way up, through the atom of the chemist and physicist, through man, through the energising Life of a planet, up to the Logos, the deity of our solar system, the Intelligence or Life which lies back of all manifestation or of nature, and on to some greater scheme in which even our God has to play His part and to find His place. It is a wonderful picture if true.

I cannot deal tonight with the different developments of this intelligence animating all atoms, but I should like for a moment to take up what is perhaps the method of their evolution, and this from the human standpoint (which concerns us the most intimately) remembering ever that what is true of any one atom should be true in greater or less degree of all.

In considering broadly the atoms of the solar system, including the system itself, there are two things noticeable: the first is the intense life and activity of the atom itself, and its internal atomic energy; and the second is its interaction with other atoms—repulsing some and attracting others. Perhaps, then, we may deduce from these facts, that the method of evolution for every atom is due to two causes: the internal life of the atom itself, and its interaction or intercourse with other atoms. These two stages are apparent in the evolution of the human atom. The first was emphasised by the Christ when He said: "the kingdom of God is within you," thus pointing all human atoms to the centre of life or energy within themselves, and teaching them that from and through that centre they must expand and grow. Each one of us is conscious of being centred within himself; he considers everything from his own standpoint, and the outer happenings are mostly interesting just in so far as they concern himself. We deal with things as they affect us personally, and all that occurs to others at a certain stage of our evolution is important only as it concerns ourselves. That is the present stage of many, and is characteristic of the majority; it is the period of intense individualism, and that in which the "I" concept is of paramount importance. It involves much internal activity.

The second way the human atom grows is through its interaction with all other atoms, and this is something which is only just beginning to dawn upon the human intelligence, and to assume its just importance. We are only beginning to realise the relative significance of competition and of co-operation, and are on the verge of realising that we cannot live our life selfishly and apart from the group in which we find a place; we are commencing to learn that if our brother is held back, and is not making progress, and if the other human atoms are not vibrating as they should, every atom in the body corporate is affected. None of us will be complete until all other units have achieved their fullest and most complete development.

Next week I shall enlarge a little upon this, when I take up the question of form building. I only seek tonight, in bringing this lecture to a conclusion, to bring to your consciousness an appreciation of the place we each hold in the general scheme, and to enable us to realise the importance of the interaction which goes on between all atoms. I seek to point out the necessity of finding for ourselves our place in the group to which we naturally belong (in which we are as the electrons to the positive charge), and of our then proceeding to do our work within that larger atom, the group.

This makes the entire hypothesis not merely a wild dream, but a practically useful ideal. If it is true that all the cells of our bodies, for instance, are the electrons which we hold coherently together, and if we are the energising factor within the material form, it is of prime importance that we recognise that fact, and deal rightly and scientifically with those forms and their atoms. This involves the practical care of the physical body and the wise adaptation of all our energy to the work to be done, and to the nature of our objective; it necessitates the judicious utilisation of that aggregate of cells which is our instrument, or tool, and our sphere of manifestation. This is something of which we, as yet, know little. When this thought is developed, and the human being is recognised as a force centre, the attitude of people towards their work and mode of living will be fundamentally altered. The point of view of the medical world, for instance, will be changed, and people will study the right methods of utilising energy. Disease through ignorance, will no longer exist, and the methods of transmitting force will be studied and followed. We shall then be truly intelligent atoms—a thing we, as yet, are not.

Again, we shall not only be practical in the handling

of our material bodies, because we understand their constitution, but we shall consciously find our place within the group, and direct our energy to the benefiting of the *group,* and not, as now, to the furthering of our own ends. Many atoms have not only an internal life of their own, but also radiate, and as radio-activity is gradually understood, so the study of man as a centre of active radiation will also come into being. We are standing these days on the verge of wonderful discoveries; we are nearing a marvellous synthesis of the thought of the world; we are advancing towards that period when science and religion will come to the help of each other, and when philosophy will add its quota to the understanding of the truth.

The use of the imagination will frequently open up a wonderful vision, and if this imagination is based on essentials, and starts with a logical hypothesis, perhaps it will lead us to the solution of some of the mysteries and problems which are distressing the world now. If things are to us mysterious and inexplicable, may it not be because of that great Entity Who is manifesting through our planet, and Who is working out a definite purpose and plan, just as you and I may be doing in our lives. At times we carry our physical vehicle into situations, and bring about difficulties in connection with it, which are both painful and distressing; granted the hypothesis upon which we are working, it may, therefore, be logical to surmise that the great Intelligence of our planet is similarly carrying His entire body of manifestation (which includes the human family) into situations which are distressing to the atoms. Surely it may be logical to suppose that the mystery of all we see around us may be hidden in the will and intelligent purpose of that greater Life, Who works through our planet as man works through the medium of his physical body, and yet Who is Himself but an atom within a still larger sphere, which is indwelt by the solar Logos, the Intelligence Who is the sum total of all the lesser lives.

LECTURE III.

THE EVOLUTION OF FORM, OR GROUP EVOLUTION.

I want to enlarge tonight upon the basic idea of the unity of consciousness, or of intelligence, as developed somewhat in the lecture last week, and to extend the concept still further. It has been said that all evolution proceeds from homogeneous, through heterogeneity, back again to homogeneity, and it has been pointed out that:

> "Evolution is a continually accelerating march of all the particles of the universe which leads them simultaneously, by a path sown with destruction, but uninterrupted and unpausing, from the material atom to that universal consciousness in which omnipotence and omniscience are realised; in a word, to the full realisation of the Absolute of God."

This proceeds from those minute diversifications which we call molecules and atoms up to their aggregate as they are built into forms; and continues on through the building of those forms into greater forms, until you have a solar system in its entirety. All has proceeded under law, and the same basic laws govern the evolution of the atom as the evolution of a solar system. The macrocosm repeats itself in man, the microcosm, and the microcosm is again reflected in all lesser atoms.

These remarks and the previous lecture concern themselves primarily with the material manifestation of a solar system, but I shall seek to lay the emphasis in our future talks principally upon what we might call the psychical evolution, or the gradual demonstration and evolutionary unfoldment of that subjective intelligence or consciousness which lies behind the objective manifestation.

As usual, we will handle this lecture in four divisions: First, we will take the subject of the evolutionary process, which, in this particular case is the evolution of the form, or the group; then the method of group development; next we will consider the stages that are followed during the cycle of evolution, and finally we will conclude with an attempt to be practical, and to gather out of our conclusions some lesson to apply to the daily life.

The first thing necessary for us to do is to consider somewhat the question of what a form really is. If we turn to a dictionary we will find the word defined as follows: "the external shape or configuration of a body." In this definition the emphasis is laid upon its externality, upon its tangibility and exoteric manifestation. This thought is also brought out if the root meaning of the word 'manifestation' is carefully studied. It comes from two Latin words, meaning "to touch or handle by the hand" (*manus,* the hand, and *fendere,* to touch), and the idea then brought to our minds is the triple thought that that which is manifested is that which can be felt, contacted, and realised as tangible. Yet in both these interpretations the most vital part of the concept is lost sight of, and we must look elsewhere for a truer definition. To my mind, Plutarch conveys the idea of the manifestation of the subjective through the medium of the objective form in a much more illuminating way than does the dictionary. He says:—

> "An idea is a being incorporeal, which has no subsistence by itself, but gives figure and form unto shapeless matter, and becomes the cause of manifestation."

Here you have a most interesting sentence, and one of real occult significance. It is a sentence which will repay careful study and consideration, for it embodies a concept that concerns itself not only with that little manifestation, the atom of the chemist and the physicist, but of all forms that are constituted by their means, including the manifestation of a human being and of the Deity of a solar system, that great Life, that all-embracing, universal Mind, that vibrant centre of energy, and that great enfolding consciousness Whom we call God, or Force, or the Logos, the *Existence* Who is expressing Himself through the medium of the solar system.

In the Christian Bible the same thought is borne out by St. Paul in a letter to the Church at Ephesus. In the second chapter of the Epistle to the Ephesians he says: "We are his workmanship." Literally, the correct translation from the Greek is: "We are his poem, or idea," and the thought in the mind of the apostle is that through the medium of every human life, or in the aggregate of lives which compose a solar system, God is, through the form, whatever it may be, working out an idea, a specific concept, or detailed poem. A man is an embodied thought, and this is also the concept latent in the definition of Plutarch. You have therein first the idea of a selfconscious entity, you have then to recognise the thought or purpose which that entity is seeking to express, and finally, you have the body or form which is the sequential result.

The term Logos, translated as the Word, is frequently used in the New Testament, in speaking of the Deity. The outstanding passage in which this is the case is the first chapter of St. John's Gospel, where the words occur: "In the beginnig was the Word, and the Word was with God, and the Word was God." Let us consider for a minute the meaning of the expression. Its literal translation is 'the

Word', and it has been defined as "the rendering in objective expression of a concealed thought." If you take any noun, or similar word, for instance, and study its objective significance, you will find that always a definite thought is conveyed to the mind, involving purpose, intent, or perhaps some abstract concept. If this same method of study can be extended to include the idea of the Deity or the Logos, much light may be gained upon this abstruse question of the manifestation of God, the central Intelligence, by the means of the material form, whether we see Him manifested through the tiny form of a chemical atom, or that gigantic physical body of His we call a solar system.

We found in our lecture last week that there was one thing that could be predicated of all atoms, and that scientists everywhere were coming to recognise one distinguishing characteristic. They have been shown to possess symptoms of mind and a rudimentary form of intelligence. The atom demonstrates the quality of discrimination, of selective power, and of ability to attract or repulse. It may seem curious to use the word *intelligence* in connection with an atom of chemistry, for instance, but nevertheless the root meaning of the word embodies this idea perfectly. It comes from two Latin words: *inter*, between, and *legere* to choose. Intelligence, therefore, is the capacity to think or choose, to select, and to discriminate. It is, in reality, that abstract, inexplicable something which lies back of the great law of attraction and repulsion, one of the basic laws of manifestation. This fundamental faculty of intelligence characterises all atomic matter, and also governs the building up of forms, or the aggregation of atoms.

We have earlier dealt with the atom *per se*, but have in no way considered its building into form, or into that totality of forms which we call a kingdom in nature. We have considered somewhat the essential nature of the atom, and its prime characteristic of intelligence, and have laid our emphasis upon that out of which all the different forms as we know them, are built, all forms in the mineral kingdom, in the vegetable kingdom, in the animal kingdom, and in the human. In the sum total of all forms you have the totality of nature as generally understood.

Let us now extend our idea from the individual forms that go to the constitution of any of these four kingdoms of nature, and view them as providing that still greater form which we call the kingdom itself, and thus view that kingdom as a conscious unit, forming a homogeneous whole. Thus each kingdom in nature may be considered as providing a form through which a consciousness of some kind or grade can manifest. Thus also, the aggregate of animal forms composes that greater form which we designate the kingdom itself, and this animal kingdom likewise has its place within a still greater body. Through that kingdom a conscious life may be seeking expression, and through the aggregate of kingdoms a still greater subjective Life may be seeking manifestation.

In all these kingdoms which we are considering—mineral, vegetable, animal and human—we have three factors again present, provided, of course, that the basis of our reasoning is correct: first, that the original atom is itself a life: secondly, that all forms are built up of a multiplicity of lives, and thus a coherent whole is provided through which a subjective entity is working out a purpose: thirdly, that the central life within the form is its directing impulse, the source of its energy, the origin of its activity, and that which holds the form together as a unity.

This thought can be well worked out in connection with man, for instance. For the purposes of our lecture, man can be defined as that central energy, life, or intelligence, who works through a material manifestation or form, this form being built up of myriads of lesser lives. In this connection a curious phenomenon has been frequently noticed at the time of death; it was brought very specially to my notice some years ago by one of the ablest surgical nurses of India. She had for a long time been an atheist, but had begun to question the ground of her unbelief after several times witnessing this phenomenon. She stated to me that, at the moment of death, in several cases, a flash of light had been seen by her issuing from the top of the head, and that in one particular case (that of a girl of apparently very advanced spiritual development and great purity and holiness of life) the room had appeared to be lit up momentarily by electricity. Again, not long ago, several of the leading members of the medical profession in a large middle west city were approached by an interested investigator, by letter, and asked if they would be willing to state if they had noted any peculiar phenomena at the moment of death. Several replied by saying that they had observed a bluish light issuing from the top of the head, and one or two added that they had heard a snap in the region of the head. In this last instance we have a corroboration of the statement in Ecclesiastes, where the loosing of the silver cord is mentioned, or the breaking of that magnetic link which unites the indwelling entity or thinker to his vehicle of expression. In both the types of cases above mentioned can apparently be seen an ocular demonstration of the withdrawal of the central light or life, and the consequent disintegration of the form, and the scattering of the myriad lesser lives.

It may therefore seem to some of us a logical hypothesis that just as the atom of chemistry is a tiny sphere, or form, with a positive nucleus, which holds rotating around it the negative electrons, so all forms in all the kingdoms of nature are of a similar structure, differing only in degree of consciousness or intelligence. We can therefore regard the kingdoms themselves as the physical expression of some great subjective life, and can by logical steps come to the recognition that every unit in the human family is an atom in the body of that greater unit who has been called in some of the Scriptures the "Heavenly Man." Thus we arrive finally at the concept that the solar system is but the aggregate of all kingdoms and all forms, and the Body of a Being Who is expressing Himself through it, and utilising it in order to work out a definite purpose and central idea. In all these extensions of our final hypothesis, the same triplicity can be seen; an informing Life or Entity manifesting through a form, or a multiplicity of forms, and demonstrating discriminative intelligence.

It is not possible to deal with the method whereby the forms are built up, or to enlarge upon the evolutionary process by means of which atoms are combined into forms, and the forms themselves collected into that greater unit which we call a kingdom in nature. This method might be briefly summed up in three terms—*involution,* or the involving of the subjective life in matter, the method whereby the indwelling Entity takes to itself its vehicle of expression; *evolution,* or the utilisation of the form by the subjective life, its gradual perfecting, and the final liberating of the imprisoned life; and the *law of attraction and repulsion,* whereby matter and spirit are co-ordinated, whereby the central life gains experience, expands its consciousness, and, through the use of that particular form attains self-knowledge and self-control. All is carried forward under this basic law. In every form you have a central life, or idea, coming into manifestation, involving itself more and more in substance, clothing itself in a form and shape adequate to its need and requirement, utilising that form as a means of expression, and then—in due course of time—liberating itself from the environing form in order to acquire one more suited to its need. Thus through every grade of form, spirit or life progresses, until the path of return has been traversed, and the point of origin achieved. This is the meaning of evolution and here lies the secret of the cosmic incarnation. Eventually spirit frees itself from form, and attains liberation plus developed psychical quality and graded expansions of consciousness.

We might look at these definite stages, and study them very cursorily. We have in the first case the process of involution. This is the period in which the limiting of the life within the form or sheath proceeds, and it is a long slow process, covering millions upon millions of years. This great cycle is participated in by every type of life. It concerns the life of the Solar Logos manifesting through a solar system. It is part of the life cycle of the planetary Spirit manifesting through such a sphere as our Earth planet; it includes that life which we call human, and sweeps into the path of its energy the tiny life which functions through an atom of chemistry. It is the great process of *becoming*, and that which makes existence and *being* itself possible. This period of limitation, of a gradually increasing imprisonment, and of an ever deeper descent into matter, is succeeded by one of adaptation, in which the life and the form become intimately inter-related, and subsequent to this is the period wherein that inner relation becomes perfected. The form is then adequate to the needs of the life, and can be utilised. Then, as the life within grows and expands, it is paralleled by the crystallisation of the form, which no longer suffices as a means of expression. Following upon crystallisation, we have the period of disintegration. Limitation, adaptation, utilisation, crystallisation, and disintegration,—these are the stages which cover the life of any entity, or embodied idea of greater or less degree, which seeks expression through matter.

Let us carry out this thought in connection with the human being. The process of limitation can be seen in the taking of a physical form, and in those early rebellious days, when a man is full of desires, aspirations, longings and ideals, which he seems unable to express or to satisfy. Then comes the period of adaptation, wherein the man begins to utilise what he has, and to express himself as best he may through the medium of those myriads of lesser lives and intelligences which constitute his physical, his emotional, and his mental bodies. He energises his threefold form, forcing it to carry out his behests and fulfil his purposes, and thus carry out his plan, whether for good or evil. This is succeeded by the stage in which he utilises the form as far as in him lies, and comes to what we call maturity. Finally, in the later stages of life, we have the crystallisation of the form, and the man's realisation of its inadequacy. Then comes the happy release which we call death, that great moment in which the "spirit in prison" escapes from the confining walls of its physical form. Our ideas about death have been erroneous; we have looked upon it as the great and ultimate terror, whereas in reality it is the great escape, the entrance into a fuller measure of activity, and the release of the life from a crystallised vehicle and an inadequate form.

Thoughts similar to these can be worked out in connection with all forms, and not only with those in connection with the physical body of a human being. These ideas can be applied to forms of government, forms of religion, and forms of scientific or philosophical thought. It can be seen working out in a peculiarly interesting manner in this cycle in which we live. Everything is in a state of flux; the old order changeth, and a period of transition is in progress; the old forms, in every department of thought, are disintegrating, but only in order that the life which gave them being may escape, and build for itself that which will be more satisfactory and adequate. Take, for instance, the old religious form of the Christian faith. Here I must warn you not to misunderstand me. I am not trying to prove that the spirit of Christianity is inadequate, and I am not seeking to demonstrate that its well-tried and well-proven truths are erroneous. I am only trying to point out that the form through which that spirit seeks to express itself has somewhat served its purpose, and is proving a limitation. Those same great truths, and those same basic ideas, require a more adequate vehicle through which to function. Christian thinkers at this time need to distinguish very carefully between the vital truths of Christianity, and the crystallised form of theology. The living impulse was given by the Christ. He enunciated these great and eternal truths, and sent them forth to take form and meet the need of a suffering world. They were limited by the form, and there came a long period wherein that form (religious dogmas and doctrines) gradually grew and took shape. Centuries ensued wherein the form and the life seemed adapted to each other, and the Christian ideals expressed themselves through the medium of that form. Now the period of crystallisation has set in, and the expanding Christian consciousness is finding the limitations of the theologians inadequate and restricting. The great fabric of dogmas and doctrines, as built up by the churchmen and theologians of the ages, must inevitably disintegrate, but only in order that the life within may escape, build for itself a better and more satisfactory means of expression, and thus measure up to the mission upon which it was sent.

In the different schools of thought everywhere the same thing can be seen. All of them are expressing some idea by means of a particular form, or set of forms, and it is very necessary for us to remember that the triple life back of all forms is nevertheless but One, though the vehicles of expression are diverse, and ever prove inadequate as time elapses.

What, then, is the purpose back of this endless process of form building, and this combining of the lesser forms? What is the reason of it all, and what will prove to be the goal? Surely it is the development of quality, the expansion of the consciousness, the development of the faculty of realisation, the production of the powers of the psyche, or the soul, the evolution of intelligence. Surely it is the gradual demonstration of the basic idea or purpose which that great Entity Whom we call the Logos, or God, is working out through the solar system. It is the demonstration of His psychic quality, for God is intelligent Love; and the fulfilment of His determined purpose, for God is intelligent loving Will.

For all the different grades and types of atoms there is a goal and a purpose also. There is a goal for the atom of chemistry; there is a point of achievement for the human atom, man; the planetary atom also will some day demonstrate its basic purpose, and the great Idea which lies back of the solar system will some day be revealed. Is it possible for us in a few brief moments of study to get a sound conception of what that purpose may be? Perhaps we can get some broad, general idea, if we approach the subject with sufficient reverence and sensitiveness of outlook, bearing carefully in mind always that only the ignorant dogmatise, and only the unwise deal in detail when considering these stupendous topics.

We have seen that the atom of chemistry, for instance, demonstrates the quality of intelligence; it shows symptoms of discriminative mind, and the rudiments of selective capacity. Thus the tiny life within the atomic form is demonstrating psychic quality. The atom is then built into all the different forms at varying times and stages, and each time it gains somewhat according to the force and life of the entity who ensouls that form, and preserves its homogeneity. Take, for instance, the atom that goes to the building of a form in the mineral kingdom; it shows not only discriminative selective mind, but elasticity. Then in the vegetable kingdom these two qualities appear, but a third is also found, which we might call sensation of a rudimentary kind. The initial intelligence of the atom has acquired something during the transition from form to form and from kingdom to kingdom. Its responsiveness to contact, and its general awareness have increased. When we come to the study of the evolution of consciousness we can take this up in greater detail; all I am endeavouring to do tonight is to show that in the vegetable kingdom forms built up of atoms show not only discriminative intelligence and elasticity, but also are capable of sensation, or of that which, in the vegetable kingdom, corresponds to emotion or feeling, emotion being but rudimentary love. Next we have the animal kingdom, in which the animal forms show not only all the above qualities, but to them is added instinct, or that which will some day blossom into mentality. Finally, we come to the human being, who shows all these qualities in far greater degree, for the fourth kingdom is but the macrocosm for the three lower. Man demonstrates intelligent activity, he is capable of emotion or love, and has added yet another factor, that of intelligent will. He is the deity of his own little system; he is not only conscious, but he is selfconscious. He builds his own body of manifestation, just as does the Logos, only on a tiny scale; he controls his little system by the great law of attraction and repulsion, as does the Logos, and he energises it and synthesises his threefold nature into a coherent unit. He is the three in one, and the one in three, just as is the Logos.

There is a future for every atom in the solar system. Before the ultimate atom there lies a tremendous goal, and as the aeons slip away the life that animates that atom will pass through all the varying kingdoms of nature until it find its goal in the human kingdom.

The idea might now be extended somewhat, and we might consider that great Entity Who is the informing life of the planet, and Who holds all the different kingdoms of nature within His consciousness. May it not be possible that His intelligence, as it informs the totality of all groups and kingdoms, is the goal for man, the human atom? Perhaps as time progresses the scope of his present realisation may also be ours, and for His, as for all those great Lives Who inform the planets of the solar system, there may be the attainment of that tremendous reach of consciousness which characterises that great Existence Who is the ensouling Life of the solar system. May it not be true that among the different grades of consciousness, extending, for instance, from the atom of the chemist and physicist, up to the Logos of the solar system, there are no gaps, and no abrupt transitions, but there is ever a gradual expansion and a gradual evolution from one form of intelligent manifestation to another, and always the life within the form gains in *quality* by means of the experience.

When we have built this idea into our consciousness,

when it is apparent to us that there is purpose and direction underlying everything, when we realise that not a single thing occurs that is not the outcome of the conscious will of some entity, and that all that happens has a definite aim and goal, then we have the clue to ourselves, and to all that we see happening around us in the world. If, for instance, we realise that we have the building up and care of our physical bodies, that we have the control of our emotional nature, and the responsibility for the development of our mentality, if we realise that we are the energising factors within our bodies, and that when we withdraw from those bodies they disintegrate and fall to pieces; then perhaps we have the clue to what the informing Life of the planet may be doing, as He works through forms of every kind (continents, civilisations, religions, and organisations) upon this earth; to what has gone on in the moon, which is now a disintegrating form, to what is going on in the solar system, and to what will happen in the solar system when the Logos withdraws from that which is, for Him, but a temporary manifestation.

Let us now make practical application of these thoughts. We are living at this time in a period in which all the forms of thought seem breaking up, in which the religious life of the peoples is no longer what it was, in which dogma and doctrine of every kind come under criticism. Many of the old forms of scientific thought are likewise disintegrating, and the foundations of the old philosophies seem to be shaken. Our lot is cast in one of the most difficult periods of the world's history, a period which is characterised by the breakup of nations, the smashing of old relationships and ties, and the apparently imminent disruption of civilisation. We need to encourage ourselves by remembering that all this is occurring just because the life within those forms is becoming so strong that it finds them a prison and a limitation; and we must recollect that this transition period is the time of the greatest promise that the world has ever seen. There is no room for pessimism and despair, but only for the profoundest optimism. Many today are upset and distraught because the foundations seem to be shaken, the carefully reared and deeply cherished structures of religious thought and belief, and of philosophical finding seem in danger of falling, yet our anxiety exists simply because we have been too much engrossed with the form, and too much occupied with our prison, and if disruption has set in, it is only in order that the life may build for itself new forms and thereby evolve. The work of the destroyer is as much the work of God as that of the constructor, and the great god of destruction has to smash and rend the forms in order that the work of the builder may become possible, and the spirit able more adequately to express itself.

To many of us these ideas may seem novel, fantastic, and untenable. Yet even if they are only hypotheses, they may prove interesting and give us a possible clue to the mystery. We see civilisations disrupted, we see the religious fabrics tottering, we see philosophies successfully attacked, we see the foundations of material science shaken. Yet, after all, what are civilisations? What are the religions? What are the great races? Simply the forms through which the great threefold central Life, Who informs our planet, seeks to express Himself. Just as we express ourselves through the medium of a physical, an emotional, and a mental nature, so He expresses Himself through the totality of the kingdoms of nature, and through the nations, races, religions, sciences and philosophies, in existence at this time. As His life pulsates through every department of His being we, as cells and atoms within that greater manifestation, follow each transition, and are swept along from one stage to another. As time progresses, and our consciousness expands, we shall enter more and more into a knowledge of His plan as He is working it out, and shall eventually be in a position to collaborate with Him in His essential purpose.

To sum up the central thought of this lecture: Let us endeavour to realise that there is no such thing as inorganic matter, but that every atom is a life. Let us realise that all forms are living forms, and that each is but the vehicle of expression for some indwelling entity. Let us seek to comprehend that this is likewise true of the aggregate of all forms. Thus we have the clue to ourselves, and perhaps the clue to the mystery of the solar system.

LECTURE IV.

THE EVOLUTION OF MAN, THE THINKER.

This is the fourth in the series of talks which we have had the past month, and perhaps by means of them we have been able to get an idea of one of the fundamental principles which underly evolution, and which can be seen working out in the solar system.

Let us first briefly recapitulate, in order that we may approach our subject tonight with certain ideas clearly formulated. We have seen that our interpretation of the processes of nature necessitates a threefold concept, which concerns itself with the life aspect, with the substance aspect, and with their close interrelation through the faculty of intelligence manifesting as consciousness of some kind or other. This interrelation will produce, finally, the perfected expression (through the medium of matter) of the conscious purpose of some indwelling entity. I seek to emphasise the fact that the goal of my endeavour is to put before you a hypothesis and a suggestion which may have within it the germ of a possible truth, and which seems to some of us the clearest way of explaining the mystery of the universe. We have seen that the three parts of the one great whole are Spirit, or Life, manifesting through a second factor which we call substance or matter, and utilising a third factor, which we call the intelligence. In the gradual synthesis of these three component aspects of deity can be seen the evolution of consciousness.

We next arrived at a more technical discussion of the subject of substance itself, dealing not with the differentiated substances or elements, but with the concept of a primordial substance, and endeavouring to get back as far as possible toward that which has been called by Sir William Crookes "protyle", or that which lies back of the tangible, or objective. We considered the atom, and found that its latest definition was that it was in reality a unit of force or energy consisting of a positive charge of electricity energising a number of negative particles. It became apparent to us that the tiny atom of the chemist and the physicist was within itself a solar system, with the same general conformation as the greater system, demonstrating a similar activity and governed by analogous laws. We found that it had a central sun, and that around this central sun, pursuing their definite orbits, might be seen the electrons. We noted, also, the fact that the elements differ only according to the number and the arrangement of these electrons around the central positive charge. From this we passed on to the consideration of the soul, or the psyche, of the atom, and found that scientists recognise the truth that atoms themselves possess quality, show symptoms of mind or intelligence, and can discriminate, select, and choose.

We then proceeded to weave what appeared to be a fairytale. We pictured the human being as an atom, and traced the resemblance of man to an atom; we found that he attracted and held within his sphere of influence the matter of his various bodies, mental, emotional and physical, in exactly the same way as the electrons were held revolving around their central focal point. The idea proved capable of still further expansion, and we turned our attention to the planet, picturing it as similar in its nature to the human atom, and to the ultimate atom of substance, being but the expression of a life manifesting through a spheroidal form and working out an intelligent purpose. Then we reached our consummation, and viewed the solar system as a cosmic atom, energised by the life of the Logos.

We have, therefore, under consideration, four kinds of atoms:

First, the atom of the chemist and physicist.
Secondly, the human atom, or man.
Thirdly, the planetary atom, energised by a planetary Logos, or the Heavenly Man.
Fourthly, the solar atom, indwelt by the solar Logos, or the Deity.

If we are right in our fundamental concept, if there is a grain of reality in our hypothesis, and if there is a substratum of truth in our idea of the atom from which the elements are compounded, it is to be recognised as a life working intelligently through the medium of a form. Then it can perhaps be proven that man is equally a life or centre of energy, manifesting through his bodies; then it can perhaps be demonstrated that a planet is also the medium of expression of a still greater centre of energy, and further, under the law of analogy, it may perhaps be proven at some distant time that there is a God or central life back of material nature, and an Entity Who functions consciously through the solar system.

At our last lecture we took up another phase of manifestation. We studied the atom itself, and considered it as it entered into relationship with other atoms, and through their mutual coherence formed groups or congeries of atoms. In other words, we considered the atom as it was built into the different forms in the various kingdoms of nature, and found that, in the process of evolution, atoms themselves gravitate towards other and greater central points, becoming in their turn electrons. Thus, every form is but an aggregate of smaller lives.

Very briefly then we touched upon the different kingdoms of nature, and traced the development of the soul, or the psyche in all of them. Of the atom we have already predicated intelligence, or discriminative power, and we found that in the building up of forms in the mineral, vegetable, and animal kingdoms what we understand as sensation begins to appear, and we then have the rudiments of embryonic emotion, or feeling—the physical plane reflection of love. Thus we have one aspect of the threefold nature of God, intelligence, demonstrating through the atom; and through the form we have the love, or attractive quality manifesting. This can also be expressed in the recognition that in these two aspects of the central divine life you have the third person of the Logoic Trinity co-operating with the second; you have the intelligent activity of divinity, or the Holy Spirit aspect, working in connection with the second aspect, or the Son, Who is the builder of forms. This is brought out in an interesting manner in Proverbs viii. where Wisdom cries aloud (Wisdom in the Old Testament representing the Christ aspect), and after pointing out that He was with God before ever there was creation, goes on to say that when "He appointed the foundations of the earth, then I was by Him as the master worker or builder". Students would do well to study this chapter in connection with the ideas that we are here formulating, being careful to ascertain the exact translation.

We now come to the consideration of our subject for tonight, that of the evolution of man, the thinker. We shall see that in man comes in another aspect of divinity. Browning, in Paracelsus, covers the subject that we have been considering in a most interesting manner, summing it up as follows:

"Thus He (God) dwells in all,
To man—the consummation of this scheme
Of being, the completion of this sphere
Of life: whose attributes had here and there
Been scattered o'er the visible world before,
Asking to be combined, dim fragments meant
To be united in some wondrous whole,
Imperfect qualities throughout creation,
Suggesting some one creature yet to make,
Some point where all those scattered rays should meet
Convergent in the faculties of man."

Having therefore discovered two aspects of divinity in the atom and in the form, we shall find the triplicity perfected in man. We have been told that man is made in the image of God, and we would therefore expect to see him reflecting the threefold nature of the Logos. He must demonstrate intelligence, he must show forth love, and he must manifest will. Let us consider some of the definitions of man as found in the dictionary and elsewhere. The definition found in the Standard Dictionary is a profoundly uninteresting one, and is as follows:— Man is "an individual of the human race", and then follows a long list of suggestive derivations of the word man, running through every known tongue, and concluding with the statement that many of them are improbable. That derivation which ascribes the definition of man to the Sanskrit root 'man', the one who thinks, is to my mind the most satisfying. Mrs. Besant, in one of her books, gives an exceptionally clear definition as follows: "Man is that being in whom highest spirit and lowest matter are linked together by intelligence." Man is here pictured as the meeting place for all the three lines of evolution, spirit, matter, and linking intellect; he is shown to be the one who unifies the self, the not-self, and the relation between them, and he is seen to be the knower, that which is known, and knowledge. What is the purpose of the intellect, or of knowledge? Surely its purpose is to adapt the material form to the need and requirements of the indwelling spirit; surely it is to enable the thinker within the body to utilise it intelligently, and for some definite purpose; and surely it exists in order that the central energising unit may constructively control its negative aspect. We are all of us entities, ensouling a form, and through the intelligence endeavouring to utilise that form for a specific purpose which exists within the conscious will of the true self.

In a very old occult book—so old that the date of it cannot be ascertained—can be found a definition of man which is very illuminating, and in line with the thought that we are seeking to develop tonight. Man is there defined as: "the Life and the lives." We have seen that the atom is a life, manifesting by means of the little sphere of which it is the centre. We have seen that all forms are an aggregate of lives, built up into the mineral, vegetable, and animal kingdoms. Now we can pass to the next stage on this great ladder of evolution, and we will then find that the human being is the logical sequence that grows out of all these earlier developments. First, the primordial stuff, essentially intelligent energy; next, atomic matter, in all its varying activity forming the elemental combination; then the form, the aggregate of these atoms, up to the dweller within the form, who is not only active intelligence, not only inherent attraction and love, but is also a purposeful will. This "dweller within" took possession of the form when it had reached a certain stage of preparedness, and when the component lives had reached a certain vibratory capacity; he is now utilising it, and repeating, within his own sphere of influence, the work of the atom of matter; he demonstrates, nevertheless, not in one way, nor in two, but in three. In man, therefore, in deed and in truth, you have what the Christian would term the "image of God." For, as must be apparent to all thinkers, the only way in which we can know God is through the study of His nature, or His psychic quality. We know that God is intelligence, we know that He is love, or the great attractive force of the solar system, and we know that He is the great will or purpose back of all manifestation. In every Scripture in the world the Deity is pictured under these three aspects, and manifests through nature in this triple manner.

The evolution of substance is a thing of gradual growth; it is in time supplemented by the slow working out of the inner subjective *quality* of the life of God, and thus His essential nature is demonstrated. First, you have one aspect demonstrating, then another slowly appears, and finally the third can be seen, and you have the stupendous combination and consummation, the human being. He synthesises and blends the three aspects, uniting them in himself. He is the totality of the divine attributes, though as yet they are largely embryonic, and he has to repeat within his cycle of evolution the identical processes that the atom itself has followed. Just as the atom pursues its own internal course, and just as it also has later to be drawn into and to merge and blend with other atoms in the formation of a group, so the human atom equally has to find his place within a greater form.

Let us, therefore, consider for a little what is the method of the evolutionary process for a human being. We have seen that in him the three lines converge, and that he is a point of synthesis, with one aspect as yet predominant, that of the intelligence, with the second aspect of love-wisdom just beginning to make its presence felt, and with the highest aspect of spiritual will as yet purely embryonic.

We have, nearly all of us, been brought up in the belief in what is called "the fall of man". There are few these days who believe the story of the fall as it is given in the first chapter of Genesis, and we most of us credit it as having an allegorical interpretation. What is the occult truth underlying this curious story? Simply that the truth about the fall of the spirit into matter is conveyed by means of a picture to the infant mentality of man. The process of the converging of these lines is a twofold one. You have the descent into matter of the entity, of the central life, and the incarnation of spirit, and then you have the working up, out of matter, of that life or spirit, plus all that has been gained through the utilisation of form. By experimenting with matter, by dwelling within the form, by the energising of substance, by the going out of the Garden of Eden (the place where there is no scope for necessary development), and by the wandering of the Prodigal Son in the far country, you have the various stages which are pictured in the Christian Bible where man makes the discovery that he is not the form, but that he is the one who utilises it. He is intelligence, and therefore he is made in the image of the third Person of the Trinity; he is love, and through him the love aspect of the Deity will some day perfectly manifest, and he will be able to say with his elder Brother, the Christ, in reply to the demand "Lord, show us the Father", that "he that hath seen me hath seen the Father", for God is Love; and finally, through him the highest aspect, the will of God, will become manifest, and he will be perfect, even as his Father in heaven is perfect.

Just as in the evolution of substance three stages could be seen,—that of atomic energy, of group coherence, and of eventual synthesis,—so in the evolution of man will the same appear. You will have, in the early stages of human evolution, that which we might call the atomic stage, in which man comes to a gradual recognition that he is a selfconscious unit, with an individuality all his own. Anyone who has brought up children knows that stage well. It can be seen in that constant utterance of "my, my, my," the stage of appropriation for himself, with no thought of any other self. Children are naturally, advisedly, and wisely selfish. It is the stage of the gradual recognition of separative existence, and of the utilisation ever more potently by the human atom of its own internal atomic force. The infant human being rebels against the enforced guardianship of those who seek to protect it, and considers itself sufficient unto itself. This can be seen in the individual and the race.

Then, as life goes on, the man passes out of the atomic stage to a higher and a better one, when he becomes cognisant of his group relationships, when he becomes aware that he has group responsibilities, and that he has functions to work out with other separate atoms. The group consciousness begins to make itself felt. Thus the human atom finds its place within the group, the larger unit to which it belongs, and the love aspect begins to show itself. The man has passed out of the atomic stage into that of group coherence.

Later comes the stage when the man begins to realise that he has not only responsibilities to the group, but that there is something greater still. He realises that he is a part of a great universal life which underlies all groups, that he is not just a universal atom, that he is not just part of a group, but that, after merging his identity with the group—although never losing it—the group itself has to be blended again with the consciousness of that great Identity Who is the synthesis of them all. Thus he arrives at the final stage of intelligent appreciation of divine unity.

This triple idea can be found summed up in the Bible in a rather interesting phrase, where Jehovah says to Moses, the representative man, "I am that I am". If you split this verse into its three parts you have what I have been seeking to bring out tonight: First, the atomic consciousness, I AM; then the group, I AM THAT; a consciousness that he is not just a separated individual, not only a selfcentred unit, not only a self-conscious entity, but that he is something still greater. Man then reaches the recognition which will lead him to sacrifice his identity in the service of the group, and to merge his consciousness in that of the group. Of such a conscious union we know practically nothing as yet. This is succeeded by the still greater stage, when I AM THAT I AM will be for us not an impossible ideal, and a visionary concept, but a fundamental reality, when man in the aggregate will recognise himself as an expression of the universal life, and the group consciousness itself will be merged in that of the Aggregate of all groups.

We suppose, and we hope, that we are passing rapidly out of the atomic stage, and that our sphere of influence and interest is not bounded by our atomic wall, but that we are becoming (to use a now familiar term) radio-active. When this is the case we shall not be circumscribed and limited within our own shell, and the narrow confines of our own individual life, but we shall begin to radiate, and to contact other atoms, thus reaching the second stage, the attractive.

What, therefore, is the goal ahead for each one of us? What is the goal for these different atoms with which we are concerning ourselves? We are told in some of the old Eastern Scriptures, that the goal for the atom of substance is selfconsciousness. What is, therefore, the goal for the human atom, who is already selfconscious, who is already individualised, and guiding himself by means of his will? What lies ahead for man? Simply the expansion of his consciousness to include the consciousness of the great life, or being, in whose body he is himself a cell. Our physical body is, for instance, made up of innumerable lesser lives, or atoms, each one of them separated from its neighbour, each one of them distinguished by its own inherent activity, and each one forming a sphere which holds within its periphery other lesser spheres or electrons.

We have seen that man is the positive charge, and holds his multiplicity of atoms, or lesser lives, energised and bound together into coherent forms. At death, when the spirit aspect withdraws itself, the form disintegrates, and is dissolved, and these little conscious lives, having fulfilled their function, dissipate. The consciousness of the atom within the body is a very different thing to the consciousness of a man, and this we can realise with very little thought. If we concede that man is a cell in a greater sphere, may it not be possible that there is a consciousness which is to the man what his consciousness is to the cell in his body? Is it not possible that we may have ahead of us the achievement of that consciousness in the same sense as the atom of substance may some day achieve the consciousness of a human being? May it not be that this is what Browning had in his mind when he said: "Mankind, made up of all the single men; in such a synthesis the story ends." Here he holds up before us a concept of a greater Man, who is the synthesis or sum total of all the lesser units. Perhaps that synthesis may be the great Life, or the planetary Entity Who lies back of our planetary manifestation, and Who is the sum total of the group consciousness. I suggest that just as *selfconsciousness* is the goal for all the sub-human forms of life, and as *group consciousness,* or the consciousness of the Heavenly Man, is the goal for the human being, so for him, also, there may be a goal, and for him the achievement may be the development of *God consciousness.* So for him comes the struggle to evolve the realisation which is that of the solar Logos.

Thus can be seen the unity of consciousness from the most minute atom up to the Deity Himself. Thus opens up before us a wonderful picture, and a vista of possibility. Thus may the life of God be seen in its essential triple manifestation, working out in an ever expanding consciousness; demonstrating in the atom of substance, and expanding through the medium of form, until it finds one point of culmination in man, then proceeding on its course till it demonstrates as the planetary consciousness, which is the sum total of all the states of consciousness upon our planet, the earth, until we arrive at the fundamental basic Life, Who holds all the planetary evolutions synthesised within His greater sphere, the solar system. Thus, in summing up, we have four states of intelligent activity, which we might term consciousness, selfconsciousness, group consciousness, and God consciousness. These demonstrate through four types of atoms, first, the chemical atom and all atomic forms; secondly, the human atom; then, the planetary atom, and finally the all-encompassing solar atom. Ensouling these atomic forms can be seen manifesting all sub-human types of life, from the life of the atom of substance to the informing life of the higher animals, then that life which we call human, that of man, the thinker; next, the Heavenly Man, and then the great Life of the solar system, Whom the Christian calls God, or the Logos.

Browning expresses this idea of the gradual expansion of the consciousness of a human being into something greater and vaster in the following words:

"When all the race is perfected alike
As man, that is; all tended to mankind,
And, man produced, all has its end thus far;
But in completed man begins anew
A tendency to God. Prognostics told
Man's near approach; so in man's self arise
August anticipations, symbols, types
Of a dim splendour ever on before
In that eternal circle life pursues.
For men begin to pass their nature's bound,
And find new hopes and cares which fast supplant
Their proper joys and griefs; they grow too great
For narrow creeds of right and wrong, which fade
Before the unmeasured thirst for good: while peace
Rises within them ever more and more.
Such men are even now upon the earth
Serene amid the half-formed creatures round
Who should be saved by them and joined with them."

LECTURE V.

THE EVOLUTION OF CONSCIOUSNESS.

Last week we studied, very inadequately, the evolution of man, the thinker, the tenant of the bodies, and the one who uses them during the cycle of evolution. We saw that he was the summation of the evolutions which had preceded him. We led up to our study of that evolution in two previous lectures in which we considered first the substance, or atomic matter prior to its building up into a form, or the tiny atom before it was incorporated in a vehicle of some kind. Then we studied the building of forms by means of the great law of attraction, which gathered the atoms together, causing them to cohere and vibrate in unison, and thus producing a form, or an aggregation of atoms. We came to the recognition that in atomic substance we had one aspect of the Godhead, of the Deity, and of the central Force or energy of the solar system, manifesting under the aspect of intelligence, and we saw that in the form aspect of nature another quality of the Deity became manifest, that of love or attraction, the cohesive force which holds the form unified. Then we studied the human being, or man, and noted how in him all the three divine aspects met; and recognised man as a central will manifesting through a form composed of atoms, and demonstrating the three qualities of God, that of intelligence, of love-wisdom, and of will or power.

Today we are stepping out of the matter aspect of manifestation which we have been dealing with in the previous lectures, into the consideration of the consciousness within the form. We have seen that the atom may be regarded as the central life, manifesting through a spheroidal form, and showing the quality of mind; but the human atom may also be considered as a central positive life, utilising a form and demonstrating the different qualities we have enumerated; and then we said that, if we were right in our hypothesis about the atom, if we were right in considering the human being as an atom, then we might extend this primary conception to the planet, and say that within the planetary atom there is a great Life, manifesting through a form, and showing specific qualities whilst working out a specified aim; and we extended this same concept also to the great sphere of the solar system, and to the Deity Who indwells it.

Let us take up the question of consciousness itself, and study the problem a little and concern ourselves with the reaction of the life within the form. If I can thus give you a few general ideas in line with what has been earlier said, I shall be able to lay another stone upon the structure I am endeavouring to build.

The word *consciousness* comes from two Latin words: *con,* with; and *scio,* to know; and means literally 'that with which we know'. If you take a dictionary and look up this word you will find it defined somewhat as follows: "The state of being aware", or the condition of perceiving, the ability to respond to stimuli, the faculty of recognising contacts, and the power to synchronise vibration. All these phrases might be included in any definition of consciousness, but the one I want to lay emphasis upon this evening is that which the Standard Dictionary gives, and which I have earlier quoted. The average thinker who takes up the majority of the text-books dealing with this subject, is apt to find them very confusing, for they divide consciousness and the state of being aware into numerous divisions and subdivisions, until one is left in a state of complete bewilderment. Tonight we will only touch upon three types of consciousness, which we might enumerate as follows: Absolute consciousness, universal consciousness, and individual consciousness, and of these three it is only possible, really, to define two in any way with clarity.

Absolute consciousness, to the ordinary thinker, is practically impossible of recognition. It has been defined in one book as, "that consciousness in which everything is, the possible as well as the actual", and concerns everything that can be possibly conceived of as having occurred, or occurring, or going to occur. This is, possibly, absolute consciousness, and from the standpoint of the human being is the consciousness of God, Who contains within Himself the past, the present, and the future. What, then, is universal consciousness? It might be defined as consciousness, thinking time and space, consciousness with the idea of location and succession involved within it, or, in reality, group consciousness, the group itself forming either a greater or a lesser unit. Finally, individual consciousness may be defined as just as much of the universal consciousness as a separated unit can contact and can conceive of for itself.

Now, to understand these vague expressions—absolute, universal, and individual consciousness—it might be helpful if I endeavoured somewhat to illustrate. It might be done as follows: In our earlier lectures we have seen that we must consider the atom in the human body as a little entity, a tiny, intelligent life, and a microscopic, active sphere. Now taking that little cell as our starting point we may get, by its means, some concept of what these three types of consciousness are, by viewing them from the standpoint of the atom and man. Individual consciousness to the tiny atom in a man's body would be its own vibratory life, its own internal activity, and all that specifically concerns itself. Universal consciousness to the little cell might be considered as the consciousness of the entire physical body, viewing it as the unit which incorporates the atom. Absolute consciousness to the atom might be considered as the consciousness of the thinking man who is energising the body. That would be to the atom something so remote to its own inner internal life as to be practically inconceivable and unknown, yet it nevertheless sweeps into the line of its will the form and the atom within the form, and all that concerns them. This idea has only to be extended to man, considered as an atom or cell within the body of a great Entity, and one can then work out along similar lines this conception of a threefold consciousness. It might here be wise if we were to come down and consider more practical matters than absolute consciousness.

Occidental science is coming gradually to the conclusion of the esoteric philosophy of the East, that consciousness must be predicated not only of the animal and of the human being, but that it must be recognised also as extending through the vegetable on into the mineral kingdom, and that *self* consciousness must be regarded as the consummation of the evolutionary growth of consciousness in the three lower kingdoms. It is not possible in the short time now at my disposal, to go into that most fascinating study of the development of consciousness in the animal kingdom, in the vegetable kingdom, and its appearance also in the mineral kingdom; we should find, should we do so, that even minerals show symptoms of awareness, of reaction to stimuli; that they manifest signs of fatigue, and that it is possible to poison a mineral and to murder it, much as you can murder a human being. The fact that flowers have consciousness is being more readily recognised, and articles of very deep interest have been published on the consciousness of plants, opening up a very wide range of thought. We have seen that in atomic matter the only thing that we can safely predicate is that it shows intelligence, the power to select, and to discriminate. This is the predominant feature of consciousness as it manifests through the mineral kingdom. In the vegetable kingdom another quality appears, that of sensation or feeling of a rudimentary nature. It is responsive in a different way to the mineral. In the animal kingdom a third reaction appears; not only is the animal showing signs of sensation in greatly increased degree to the similar response in the vegetable kingdom, but it also shows signs of intellect, or embryo mind. Instinct is a recognised faculty of all animal units, and the word comes from the same root as the word "instigate." When the power to instigate begins within any animal form it is a sign that an embryo mentality is beginning to manifest. In all these kingdoms you have different grades and types of consciousness showing themselves, whilst in man you have the first symptoms of selfconsciousness, or the faculty in man whereby he becomes aware that he is a separated identity, that he is the indwelling impulse within the body, and the one who is in process of becoming aware by means of these bodies. This has been long taught in the East, and "esoteric philosophy teaches that everything lives and is conscious, but that not all life and consciousness is similar to the human", and it also emphasises the fact that "vast intervals exist between the consciousness of the atom and of the flower, between that of a flower and a man, between that of a man and a God." As Browning has said: "In man begins anew a tendency to God." He is not a God yet, but a God in the making; he is working out the image of God, and will some day produce it in perfection. He is the one who is seeking to demonstrate the subjective, divine, threefold life through the medium of the objective.

The method of the evolutionary development of consciousness in a human being is but a repetition on a higher turn of the spiral, of the two stages which we noted in the evolution of the atom, that of atomic energy and of group coherence. In the world at present can be seen the human family at the atomic stage of manifestation, leading on to a goal not yet achieved, the group stage.

If there is one thing apparent to all of us who are in any way interested in the faculty of awareness, and who are in the habit of noting that which passes around us, it is that of the different grades of mentality which we meet everywhere, and the different types of consciousness among men. We meet people who are alert, alive, aware of all that is going on, keenly conscious, responsive to thought currents of various kinds in human affairs, and conscious of contacts of every kind; then we meet people who seem to be asleep; there is apparently so little that interests them; they seem utterly unaware of contact; they are yet in a stage of inertia, and are not capable of responding to much outer stimuli; they are not mentally alive. One notices it, also, in children; some respond so quickly, while others we call stupid. It is not really that one is more or less essentially stupid than another; it is simply due to the inner stage of evolution of the child, to its more frequent incarnations, and the longer period that it has been occupied in becoming aware.

Let us now take the two stages, the atomic and the form stage, and see how the consciousness of the human being develops, bearing ever in mind that in the human atom is stored up all that has been gained in the earlier stages in the three lower kingdoms of nature. Man is the gainer by that vast evolutionary process which lies behind him. He starts with all that has been gained therein latent within him. He is selfconscious, and has before him a definite goal, the attainment of group consciousness. For the atom of substance the goal had been the attainment of selfconsciousness. For the human being the goal is a greater Consciousness, and a wider range of awareness.

The *atomic stage* which we are now considering is, for us, a peculiarly interesting one, because it is the stage in which the majority of the human family find themselves. In it we pass through the period (a most necessary one) of self-centredness, that cycle in which the man is principally concerned with his own affairs, with that which primarily interests him, and lives his own intense, internal, vibratory life. For a long period back of us, and perhaps at the present stage, (for I do not believe that many of us would feel insulted if we were not regarded as having attained perfection, or having achieved the goal) we are most of us intensely selfish, and only mentally interested in the things that are going on in the world, and then probably because our hearts are touched, and *we* do not like being uncomfortable, or we are interested because it is the fashion; and yet, in spite of this mental attitude, our whole attention is focussed upon the things which concern our own individual life. We are in the atomic stage, intensely active in connection with our own personal problems. Watch the throngs in the streets of any great city, and you will see everywhere people in the atomic stage, centred entirely in themselves, occupied only with their own business, intent upon their own pleasure getting, desirous only of having a good time, and only incidentally occupied with affairs which concern the group. This is a necessary and protective stage, and one of essential value to every unit of the human family. The realisation of this, therefore, will surely lead us all to be patient with our brothers and sisters who may so often irritate us.

What are the two factors whereby we evolve in and

out of the atomic stage. In the Orient for many ages the method of evolution has been regarded as a twofold one. A man has been taught that he evolves and becomes aware first by means of the five senses, and later through the development of the faculty of discrimination, coupled with dispassion. Here in the West we have primarily emphasised the five senses, and have not taught that discrimination which is so essential. If you watch the development of a little child you will become aware, for instance, that a baby develops the five senses in a certain ordered sequence, usually. The first sense it develops is hearing; it will move its head when there is a noise. Then the next sense to be noted is that of touch, and it begins to feel about with its little hands. The third sense which seems to awaken is that of sight. I do not mean by this that a baby cannot see, or that it is born blind, like a kitten, but it is often several weeks before a baby consciously sees and looks with recognition. The faculty has always been there, but there has been no realisation. So it is with the graded expansions of consciousness and realisations that lie ahead of man today. In these three paramount, or major senses, hearing, touch, and sight, you have a very interesting analogy to, and connection with the threefold manifestation of Deity, the self, the not-self, and the relation between. The self, occultly, hears and responds to vibration, thus realising Itself. It becomes aware of the not-self, and of its tangibility, through touch, but it is only when sight or conscious recognition comes in that the relation between the two is established. Two more senses are utilised by the self in making its contacts, those of taste and smell, but they are not so essential to the development of intelligent awareness as are the other three. Through these five senses we make every contact that it is possible to make upon the physical plane; through them we learn, we grow, we become aware, and we develop; through them all the great instincts are evolved; they are the great protective senses, not only enabling us to contact our environment, but also protecting us from that environment.

Having, then, learnt to be intelligent units by means of these five senses, and having, through their medium, expanded our consciousness, we reach a certain crisis, and another factor comes in, that of intelligent discrimination. Here I am referring to the discrimination which a selfconscious unit demonstrates. I refer to that conscious choice which you and I evidence, and which we will be forced to utilise as the power of evolution drives us on to the point where we will learn to distinguish between the self and the not-self, between the real and the unreal, between the life within the form, and the form which it uses, between the knower and that which is known. Here we have the whole object of evolution, the attainment of the consciousness of the real self through the medium of the not-self.

We pass through a long period or cycle of many lives, wherein we identify ourselves with the form, and are so one with the not-self that we recognise no difference, being entirely occupied with the things which are transient and impermanent. It is this identification with the not-self which leads to all the pain, dissatisfaction, and sorrow in the world, and yet we must remember that through this reaction of the self to the not-self we inevitably learn, and finally break loose from the impermanent and the unreal. This cycle of identification with the unreal parallels the stage of individual consciousness. As the atom of substance has to find its way into some form, and add its quota of vitality to a greater unit, so through the evolutionary development of consciousness the human atom has likewise to reach a point where it recognises its place in a greater Whole, and shoulders its responsibility in group activity. This is the stage which a great number of the human family are now approaching. Men are realising, as never before, the difference between the real and the unreal, between the permanent and the impermanent; through pain and suffering they are awakening to the recognition that the not-self suffices not, and they are searching without and also within, for that which will more adequately meet their needs. Men are seeking to understand themselves, to find the kingdom of God within themselves, and through Mental Science, New Thought, and the study of psychology they will arrive at certain realisations which will prove invaluable to the human race. The indication is therefore to be found that the *form stage* is rapidly approaching, and that men are passing out of the atomic period into something infinitely better and greater. Man is beginning to sense the vibration of that greater Life within Whose body he is but as an atom, and he is commencing, in a small way, to make a conscious response to that greater call, and to find possible channels whereby he can understand that greater Life which he senses, but as yet does not know. If he persists in this, he will find the group to which he belongs, and will then change his centre. No longer will he be limited by his own little atomic wall, but he will pass beyond it, and become, in his turn, a conscious, active, intelligent part of the greater whole.

And how is this change brought about? The atomic stage was developed by means of the five senses, and through the utilisation of the faculty of discrimination. The stage at which a man awakens to group realisation, and becomes a conscious participant in the activities of the group, is brought about in two ways, through meditation, and through a series of initiations. Now when I use the word "meditation" I do not mean what is perhaps usually understood by that word, a negative, receptive, state of mind, or a state of trance. There is much misconception these days as to what meditation really is, and there is a great deal of so called meditation which has been truly described by a person not so long ago, as "I shut my eyes, and open my mouth, and wait for something to happen." The true meditation is something that requires the most intense application of the mind, the utmost control of thought, and an attitude which is neither negative nor positive, but an equal balance between the two. In the Eastern Scriptures the man who is attempting meditation and achieving its results, is described as follows—and from a consideration of these words may come much help and illumination to us: "The Maha Yogi, the great ascetic, in whom is centred the highest perfection of austere penance and *abstract meditation,* by which the most unlimited powers are attained, marvels and miracles are worked, the highest spiritual knowledge is acquired, and *union with the great Spirit of the universe is eventually attained.*" Here this union with the group life is held to be the product of meditation, and there is no other method of attainment.

True meditation (of which the preliminary stages are concentration upon and application to any particular line of thought) will differ for different people and different types. The religious man, the mystic, will centre his attention upon the life within the form, upon God, upon Christ, or upon that which embodies for him the ideal. The business man, or the professional man, who, during his hours of work, is one-pointedly centred upon the matter he has on hand, and who keeps his attention fixed upon the particular problem he has to solve, is learning to meditate. Later on, when he comes to the more spiritual aspect of meditation, he will find that he has covered the hardest part of the road. The person who is reading a difficult book, and reads with the full force and power of his brain, getting at that which lies behind the written word, may be meditating as much as it is possible for him to meditate at this time. I say this for our encouragement, because we live in a cycle in which books about meditation are written, and many schools of meditation are found. All of them embody some aspect of the truth, and may be doing much good, but they may not embody that which is best for any particular individual. We need to find our own way of concentrating, to ascertain our own method of approach to that which lies within, and to study for ourselves this question of meditation.

I would like here to sound a word of warning. Avoid those schools and methods which combine forms of breathing exercises with meditation, which teach different types of physical postures, and teach their students to centre their attention upon physical organs or centres. Those who follow these methods are heading towards disaster, and apart from the physical dangers involved, and the risk of insanity and nervous disorders, they are occupying themselves with the form, which is limitation, and not with the spirit, which is life. The goal will not be achieved that way. For most of us the intellectual concentration which results in mind control, and the ability to think clearly and to think only that which we wish to think, must precede true meditation, which is a thing few people know much about. This true meditation, which it is impossible for me to enlarge upon here, will result in a definite change of polarisation, will open up to man ranges of experiences undreamt of hitherto, will reveal to him contacts that as yet he does not realise, and will enable him to find his place within the group. He will be no longer confined by the wall of his personal life, but will begin to merge that life within the greater whole. He will no longer be occupied with the things of selfish interest, but will give his attention to the problems of the group. He will no longer give his time to the culture of his own identity, but will seek to understand that greater Identity of which he is a part. This is really what all advanced men are beginning more or less to do. Little as the average man may realise it, great thinkers, such as Edison and others, arrive at a solution of their problems along the line of meditation. By a brooding concentration, by a constant recollection, and by strenuous application to the particular line of thought which interests them, they produce results, they tap the inner reservoirs of inspiration and of power, and bring down from the higher levels of the mental plane results which benefit the group. When we ourselves have done a certain amount of work along the line of meditation, when we are cultivating group interest and not self interest, when we have developed physical bodies that are strong and clean, and emotional bodies that are controlled, and not swayed by desire, when we have mental bodies that are our instruments and not our masters, then we shall know the true meaning of meditation.

When a man has made his contact through meditation with the group to which he belongs, and becomes, therefore, ever more and more group conscious, he is then in a position to take what are called a series of initiations. These initiations are simply expansions of consciousness, brought about with the help of Those Who have already achieved the goal, Who have already identified Themselves with the group, and Who are a conscious part of the body of the Heavenly Man. With Their assistance, and through

Their aid, a man will gradually awaken to the realisation that is Theirs.

There is great interest everywhere today in this subject of initiation, and an over-emphasis has been laid upon its ceremonial aspect. We need to remember that every great unfoldment of consciousness is an initiation. Every step forward along the path of awareness is an initiation. When an atom of substance was built into the form, it was for that atom an initiation. It became aware of another type of force, and its range of contact became wider. When the consciousness of the vegetable and animal kingdom merged, and the life passed from the lower kingdom into the higher, that was an initiation. When the consciousness of the animal expanded into that of the human being, still another great initiation took place. All the four kingdoms have been entered by an initiation, or through an expansion of consciousness. Ahead of the human family lies now the fifth, or spiritual kingdom, and it is likewise entered through a certain initiation, as can be seen by those who intelligently read their New Testament. And in all these cases these initiations have been brought about by the help of Those who already know. Thus we have within the evolutionary scheme not great gaps between one kingdom and another, and between one state of awareness and another, but a gradual development of consciousness, and one in which we, each one of us, have had and will have our share. If we can remember this universality of initiation we shall have a better proportioned point of view in connection with it. Every time that we become more aware of our environment, and our mental content is increased, it is an initiation on a tiny scale. Every time our horizon widens, and we think and see more broadly, it is an initiation, and herein to us lies the value of life itself, and the greatness of our opportunity.

One point I wish to make here is this: every initiation has to be self-initiated. That final stage when definite help is brought to us from outside sources is not achieved because there are great Beings anxious to help us, Who come to us where we are and seek to lift us. It comes to us because we have done the necessary work, and nothing can stop it coming. It is our right. Those who have achieved can and will and do aid and assist us, but Their hands are tied until we have done our share of the undertaking. Nothing therefore that we do to increase our usefulness in the world, no steps that we take to build better bodies, no effort that we make to gain selfcontrol and to equip our mental body, is ever lost; it is all something which we are adding to the total we are piling up, which will some day bring us to a great revelation, and every hourly, daily effort that we make, swells the tide of energy which will sweep us to the portal of initiation. The meaning of the word "initiation" is to "to go into." It means simply that an initiate is one who has taken the first steps into the spiritual kingdom, and has had the first series of spiritual revelations, each one of which is a key to a still greater revelation.

LECTURE VI.

THE GOAL OF EVOLUTION.

In using such a title as the Goal of Evolution, I feel extremely diffident; I realise that the only thing I can possibly attempt is to put certain suppositions before you, drawing upon my imagination. Naturally it is not possible for finite mind to accurately gauge the plan of the Deity. All that we can do is to study the history of the past, to investigate present conditions, and to ascertain somewhat racial and natural tendencies, and thus follow, as logically as may be, the various steps and stages. All that is permissible for us is to start from the solid basis of acquired facts and knowledge, then put them all together, and from their aggregate form an hypothesis as to what may be the possible goal. Beyond that it is impossible to go.

In our talks upon evolution, as I mentioned in the first lecture, we have been dealing somewhat with suppositions, and concerning ourselves with possibilities. Certain things we do know, and certain truths have been ascertained; yet even the facts of science, for instance, such as were so much spoken of and insisted upon forty years ago, are no longer regarded as facts, and are not used or promulgated as drastically and as emphatically as they were. Science itself is finding every year that its knowledge is very relative. The more a man grasps and knows, the greater is the horizon which opens up before him. Scientists are now venturing into what are the subtler planes of matter, and therefore into the realms of the unproven, and we should remember that, up till the present, science has refused to admit their existence. We are passing beyond the sphere of what has been called "solid matter", into such reams as are inferred when we speak about "centres of energy", "negative and positive force", and "electrical phenomena"; and the emphasis is being laid more and more upon quality rather than upon what has been called substance. The further we look ahead, the wider our speculations become, and the more we attempt to account for telepathic, psychic and other phenomena, the more we shall trespass into the realm of what is now the subjective and the subconscious, and the more we shall be forced to express ourselves in terms of quality or of energy.

If we succeed at all in accounting for that which is unusual, for that which is as yet inexplicable to us, and in ascertaining the reality of the occult, we shall bring about a condition which might almost be called paradoxical. We shall gradually make the subjective the objective.

Let us again briefly sum up the substance of the talks we have had during the past few weeks, and thus start with our ideas clarified. We dealt first with the atom of substance, and found that that atom was a centre of force; that it was of electrical origin, being the conjunction of a form of negative and positive energy, and that it showed psychic quality; we found it demonstrating selective capacity and discrimination. We then saw how the atom was gradually built up into differing forms; that these forms were distinguished by another quality to that of the atom, which we called attraction, response to sensation, and in reality a recognition of duality. In these two, the atom, and the form composed of atoms, we had two of the aspects of the Godhead manifested. We saw that the active intelligence, or the mind aspect of Deity, shows itself as the discriminating faculty, and that the second aspect shows itself as that cohesive attractive power which holds the form together. Next we found that man is the summation of the two previous developments of the divine life, combining atomic substance into form, whilst manifesting a third factor, that of intelligent purpose or will. That central will is the real man, the spiritual entity, who uses the form for purposes of his own. Man therefore embodies all the three aspects of the Godhead, and is verily and in truth made in the image of God. He is a synthesis. The life of the third Person in the Godhead, showing as intelligence, animates the substance of his bodies; the life of the second aspect, revealing that God is attractive love, is the force which builds up the atoms into the forms which he occupies, whilst he in essence is the will or spirit aspect. In him, therefore, pulsates the life of God the Father, God the Son, and God the Holy Spirit.

Having traced the different lines of evolution until they meet in man we proceeded to weave romances and to expand our ideas into something greater. We considered the sphere of the planet, and we said that it might perhaps be a logical hypothesis to posit that within that great atom, a planet, there might be—animating it and working through it—a Life that is expressing itself in and through and by that planet. From the planet we leapt to the solar system, and we saw that, if it were logical to deduce such facts concerning the planet, it might be equally logical to say that the solar system is a cosmic atom, a vast spheroidal form, animated by a central LIFE, which is working out, by means of that form, an ultimate purpose.

Having therefore dealt with the atom of substance, with the human atom, with the planetary atom, and with the cosmic atom, we left the discussion of the objective side of manifestation, and our speculations as to the nature of that which indwelt the form, and proceeded in our lecture last week to take up the subject of consciousness, of the evolution of the life within the form, and of the contacts made by means of it. We said that for each of these atoms there was a specific goal, that for the atom of substance there was the goal of self-consciousness; that all forms are conscious, but that all forms are not self-conscious, and that between man and the animal there was a profound distinction marking the difference between consciousness, and that self-consciousness which becomes possible when the spirit or will aspect of divinity indwells the form. For man there is a still greater consciousness or realisation to be achieved, which we call group-consciousness. Logically, then, we had to predicate for the planetary Deity of our Earth a further stage of unfoldment which we called God-consciousness, or the realisation of that Life which informs the entire sphere of the solar system, which is the goal for the planetary spirit. Finally we saw that there may be a still vaster stage of realisation to be compassed by the solar Logos, functioning through His solar system along some cosmic line inconceivable to us.

The subject that I am going to consider now is one that affects us very closely: namely, the attainment by man of that group consciousness which is his goal, and the expansions of his little consciousness until it measures up to that greater one which enfolds it. You will remember that in trying to explain the difference between self consciousness, group consciousness, and God consciousness, I illustrated it by pointing out that in the little atom of substance in the physical body, that tiny centralised life which goes to the constitution of the human form, we had a correspondence to the self-consciousness of the human being; that the life of the physical body, considering it in every one of its departments as a whole, is to that little selfcontained cell what group consciousness is to us; and that the consciousness of the real man, the informing entity within the body, is to that atom what God consciousness is to us, as inexplicable and as far removed. If we can extend this concept of the atom in our body and its relation to man, the thinker, to the human atom, regarding it as a unit within a still greater body, we may get an understanding of the radical difference between these three rays of consciousness.

There is a very interesting analogy between the evolution of the atom and of man (and I presume therefore of the planetary Deity and the solar Logos) in the two methods of unfoldment that are followed. We have seen that the atom has its own atomic life, and that every atom of substance in the solar system is likewise a little system in itself, having a positive centre, or central sun, with the electrons, or the negative aspect, revolving in their orbits around it. Such is the internal life of the atom, its self-centred aspect. We noted too, that the atom is now being studied along a newer line, that of radio-activity, and it is becoming apparent that in many cases there is an active radiation going on. Just where this discovery is going to lead it is impossible yet to tell, for the study of radio-active substances is as yet in its infancy, and little is actually known. Much of the earlier teaching of physical science has been revolutionised by the discovery of radium, and the more scientists find out, the more it becomes apparent, (as they themselves realise) that we are standing on the threshold of very great discoveries, and are on the eve of profound revelations.

In the human being, as he evolves and develops, these two stages can equally be seen. There is the early, or atomic stage, in which a man's whole centre of interest lies within himself, within his own sphere, where self-centredness is the law of his being, a necessary protective stage of evolution. He is purely selfish, and concerned primarily with his own affairs. This is succeeded by a later stage, in which a man's consciousness begins to expand, his interests begin to lie outside his own particular sphere, and the period arrives in which he is feeling for the *group* to which he belongs. This stage might be viewed as corresponding to that of radio-activity. He is now not only a self-centred life, but he is also beginning to have a definite effect upon his surroudings. He is turning his attention from his own personal selfish life, and is seeking his greater centre. From being simply an atom he is, in his turn, becoming an electron, and coming under the influence of the great central Life which holds him within the sphere of Its influence.

If this is so, we shall have analogous stages transpiring within the life of the planetary Deity, and this perhaps would account for various vicissitudes and happenings upon the planet. Often we consider the affairs of the world as due to human activity. The world war, for instance, is frequently regarded as the result of human mistakes and frailties. Perhaps this is so, for undoubtedly economic conditions and human ambitions may have been very largely concerned in bringing it about; but perhaps, also, it may have been partly due to the working out of the purpose of the great central Life, Whose consciousness is not as yet our consciousness, Who has His own plans and purposes and ideals, and Who, perhaps, also makes His experiments with life. On His vaster scale, and on His own high level, this planetary Spirit is learning to live, is learning to contact, and is likewise expanding His consciousness; He is Himself at school, just as you and I are at school. So, again, it may be with the solar system, and so with events of such magnitude that they escape our ken altogether. Perhaps there are occurrences within the solar system which may be due to the working out of the plans of the Deity or Logos, that central Life Who is the energising source of all there is within the solar system. I do not know, but it makes an interesting line of thought for us, and it does no harm to speculate if the effect is to give us a broader vision, a wider tolerance, and a greater and wiser optimism.

Having seen that the two stages of atomic activity and radio activity characterise the evolution of all atoms in the solar system, let us now see what are the different developments which may be expected as the consciousness within the human atom evolves. I should like to centre our attention upon this human type of consciousness, as it is the central evolution in the solar system. When the three aspects of the divine life are brought together—the indwelling life, or spirit, the material form, or substantial vehicle, and the factor of intelligent activity—certain specific results will eventuate. We shall have the gradual working out of consciousness of a particular kind; the development of psychic quality; the effect of the subjective life upon the material form; the utilisation of the form for certain specific ends, and the attainment by the indwelling entity of certain qualities. The true nature of the central life, be it God or man, will be manifested during a life cycle, whether solar or human. That is true of you and it is true of me; it is probably true of the planetary Logos, and if true of him, therefore also of a solar Logos.

Let us try, if we can, to follow some of the different developments in connection with our four types of atoms—the atom of substance, the human atom, the planetary atom and the cosmic atom. One of the first and most important developments will be *conscious response to every vibration* and contact, that is, the ability to respond to the not-self on every plane. Let me illustrate. I could go down to certain halls in this city, and gather together an audience composed of the unskilled labourers and illiterates. I could talk to them, and repeat what I have been saying this evening, and get no response whatever. Yet I could go down and give them a talk such as I gave ten years ago, along strictly evangelical or Gospel lines, and meet with a rapid reaction. Here the question of right or wrong does not enter in, but simply the difference in the ability of different grades and types of men at different stages of evolution to respond to contact and vibration. It simply means that certain people are at a stage where they can be reached by an emotional appeal, and dealt with along the line of their own personal salvation, being in the earlier atomic stage as yet. There is another stage which includes that, but which enables one to respond also to a more intellectual appeal, which gives one a certain amount of interest and satisfaction in such discussions as we have pursued, and which means investigation of those matters which concern the group, for instance. But both stages are equally right.

We can look at this matter from another angle: it is quite possible for us to meet great people, wonderful men and women, and fail to be impressed by them; we might pass them by without recognising them, and thus miss that which they have to give us. This happened in Palestine in connection with the Christ, two thousand years ago. Why? Because we ourselves are not yet great enough to respond to them. There is something still lacking in us, so that we are unable to realise or feel their particular vibration. I have heard it said, and I think it is very true, that if the Christ were to come down upon earth again, and walk among men as He did before, He might live His life amongst us day after day and we would not notice anything so very different in Him from the other good and unselfish people whom we know. We have not yet cultivated within ourselves the ability to respond to the divine in our brother. We usually see only that which is bad and coarse, and are cognisant principally of our brother's faults. We are insensitive, yet, to the best in people.

Another development will be that we shall be able to *function consciously* on all planes of being. We function consciously now on the physical plane, and there are a few people who are able to function equally consciously on the next subtler plane, that which is called the astral plane (a word I very much dislike, as it conveys no real meaning to our minds) or the plane of the emotional nature, on which a man is active when out of the physical body, in the hours of sleep or immediately after death. Very few human beings can function on the mental plane in fully awakened consciousness, and still fewer upon the spiritual plane. The object of evolution is that we should consciously function, with full continuity of realisation, upon the physical, emotional, and mental planes. This is the great achievement which will some day be ours. We shall then know what we do every hour of the day, and not for just about fourteen hours out of the twenty-four. At present we remain unconscious of where the real thinking entity is during the hours of sleep. We do not know what his activities are, nor the condition of his environment. Some day we shall utilise and employ every minute of every hour of every day.

Another purpose of evolution is a three-fold one, and it is that we should have purpose or *will, love, and energy co-ordinated.* That is not so as yet. We have much intelligent energy continuously displayed now, but it is very rare indeed to meet a person whose whole life is animated by a central purpose, which is followed unswervingly, and which is animated and instigated by love working through intelligent activity. The time is coming, however, when we shall have expanded our consciousness to such an extent, and be so active within ourselves, that we shall become radio-active. We shall then carry forward a definite purpose which will be the outcome of love, and attain our objective by means of the intelligence. This is all that God is doing, is it not? At our present stage of development, we are certainly intelligent, but as yet there is very little love. We may have a little love for those we contact or meet, and a greater love for our family and immediate friends, but we know practically nothing of group love. When group love is voiced for us by the great idealists of the race it is nevertheless true that we have reached the stage where we can respond somewhat to it, and feel that it is something we should like to see realised. It is good to remember that the more we think along such definitely altruistic lines, the more we shall build up something of very great value, and develop by slow and laborious degrees the rudiments of a real group consciousness, which as yet lies far ahead for most of us.

There are several other developments during the evolutionary process with which we might deal, and which are at present so far ahead that they are practically inconceivable unless we have the peculiar type of brain that can think somewhat abstractly. There is the stage in which we can *transcend time and space,* when the consciousness of the group in all parts of the planet, for instance, will be our consciousness, and when it will be just as easy for us to contact the consciousness of a friend in India, Africa, or elsewhere, as it is here; distance and separation will prove no barrier to intercourse. Symptoms of this can be seen in the ability which some people have to communicate telepathically, or to psychometrise.

It is all very well to spend some time visioning this distant goal, and picturing the achievement of the Logos billions of years hence, but the thing of vital interest for us is to get some idea of the immediate stage ahead; and to understand what we may expect to happen in connection with the evolutionary process during the next few thousand years. Let us consider this idea somewhat. There are, as we know, three main lines of thought in the world, the scientific, the religious, and the philosophical. Now, in these three what have we got? In the scientific line of thought we have embodied all that concerns matter, the substance aspect of manifestation; it deals with objectivity, and with that which is material, tangible, and seen; literally, with that which can be proven. In religious thought we have that which is concerned with the life within the form, which deals with the return of spirit to its source, plus all that has been gained by the use of the form; it has reference to the subjective side of nature. In philosphical thought we have what I might call the utilisation of the intelligence by the indwelling life, in order that the form may be adequately adapted to its need. Let us consider in this connection certain developments which may be looked for in the immediate future, remembering that all that I say is only intended to be suggestive, and that I speak in no dogmatic spirit.

It is obvious to most thinkers that science, having begun the study of radio-activity, is on the verge of discovering what is the nature of the power within the atom itself; it is very probable that before long we shall harness the energy of atomic matter for every conceivable purpose, for heating, for lighting, and for what I might call the motivation of everything that is carried on in the world. That force, as some of us know, was nearly discovered in the United States fifty years ago by a man called Keely, but he was not allowed to give it out to the world because of the danger thereby involved. Men are as yet far too selfish to be trusted with the distribution of atomic energy. That discovery will probably parallel the development of group consciousness. Only when man becomes radio-active and can work and think in group terms, will it be safe or wise for him to utilise the power latent in the atom. Everything in nature is beautifully co-ordinated, and nothing can be discovered or utilised before the right time. Only as man becomes unselfish will this tremendous power be permitted to pass into his hands. Nevertheless, we can, I believe, look to science to make tremendous strides in the comprehension of atomic energy.

Then paralleling the evolution of the human being again, we can look for man to dominate the air. There is a great vibratory sphere, or plane, in the solar system, called in some occult books the intuitional plane; it is called in the Eastern literature the Buddhic plane, and its symbol is the air. Just as man is beginning to find his way through the development of the intuition on to that plane now, so science is beginning to discover how to dominate the air, and as the intuition in man develops and grows, so will his control of the air be developed and grow. Another thing we can look for (and it is already being recognised somewhat) is the development of the ability to see in subtler matter. Everywhere there are children being born who see more than you or I can. I am here referring to something that is based purely on material grounds, and concerns the physical eye. I refer to etheric vision, which is seeing in the finer matter of the physical plane, or in that which is called the ethers. Much interesting work has been done along this line by students and scientists in California. Dr. Frederick Finch Strong has been working along this line in a valuable way, and teaching that the physical eye is capable of seeing etherically, and that etheric vision is the normal function of the eye. What will the development of this faculty mean? It will mean that science will have definitely to readjust its point of view as to the subtler planes. If there come within the range of vision of the normal man or woman within the next one hundred years certain aspects and forms of life that have been regarded hitherto as imaginary, we have broken once and for all that rank materialism which has distinguished us for so long, and if that which is now invisible is recognised along any particular line, who shall say how far forward it will be possible for us to go as time progresses? Again, the whole trend of evolution is toward synthesis. As we go down into matter, as we tend toward materialisation, we shall have heterogeneity; as we work back towards spirit we shall tend towards unity; so that in the religious world we can look for unity to make its appearance. There is, even now, a much greater spirit of tolerance abroad than was the case fifty years ago; but the time is rapidly approaching when the great fundamental unity that underlies all the different religions, and the fact that each faith is a necessary part of one great whole, will be recognised by men everywhere, and through this recognition, we shall have the simplification of religion. We shall have the great central facts emphasized and utilised, and the small and petty differences of organisation, and of explanation, overlooked.

Again, we can look for a very interesting happening in connection with the human family to take place, for the moment that group consciousness becomes, on a large scale, the conscious objective of man, what will occur? You will have man putting his foot upon what is called in the religious world, the PATH. You will have him definitely taking himself in hand, endeavouring to live the life of the spirit, refusing any longer to live a selfcentred atomic life; you will have him searching for his place within the greater whole, finding it by means of definite self-initiated endeavour, and then unifying himself with that group. This is all that is really meant by the teaching given about the Path in the Protestant, Catholic, and Buddhist churches. They all teach the treading of this Path; calling it by different names, such as the Way, the noble Eight-fold Path, the Path of Illumination, or the Path of Holiness. Yet it is the one Path, that which shineth ever more and more unto the perfect day.

We can look, too, for the development of the power to think abstractly, and for the awakening of the intuition. As the great races have succeeded one another upon the planet, there has ever been an ordered, directed unfoldment of the powers of the soul, and a definitely planned sequence. In the third root race, the Lemurian, the physical aspect of man was carried to a high stage of perfection. Later in the great race which preceded ours, the Atlantean, and which perished in the flood, the emotional nature of man was developed. Then in the race to which we belong, the Aryan, or fifth race, the development of the concrete, or lower mind, is the goal, and this we are developing each decade. A few are also beginning to develop the power to think in abstract terms.

When this is the case we shall see more of that peculiar, interesting capacity which some people evince, and which we call the ability to be inspired. I am not here speaking of mediumship, nor do I mean mediumistic ability. There is nothing more dangerous than that which is usually meant by the term of "medium." The average medium is a man of a negative, or receptive nature, and usually so loosely co-ordinated in his threefold nature that an extraneous force or entity can use his brain, his hand, or his body. It is quite a common phenomenon. Automatic writing, ouija boards, and spiritualistic seances of a low order, are rampant these days, and are driving thousands into insanity, or into nervous disorders. But there is something of which mediumship is simply a distortion, and this something is *inspiration.* To be capable of being inspired means that a human being has reached a stage in his evolution where he is consciously and positively under the control of his own higher self, the God within. That inner ruler, the real self, can, by definite contact, control his physical brain, and enable the man to make decisions, and to understand the truth, apart from the reasoning faculty altogether; this inner God can enable the man to speak, to write, and to pass on the truth without the use of the lower mind. Truth lies within ourselves. When we can contact our own inner God all truth will be revealed to us. We shall be Knowers. But this is a positive, not a negative thing, and means the putting of oneself in direct conscious alignment with one's Ego, or higher self, and not the throwing open of one's personality to any passing entity or spook.

This can be seen occurring now, occasionally, but it is not very often that the average man comes in contact with his higher self. Only in our moments of highest endeavour, only at the great crises of our lives, and only as the result of long discipline and strenuous meditation does this occur. But some day we shall govern our entire lives, not from the personal, selfish point of view, but from the point of view of the God within, Who is a direct revelation of Spirit on the highest plane.

The final thing I seek to bring out tonight is that the goal for each one of us is the *development of the powers of the soul,* or of the psyche. This means that you and I are going to be psychics. But I am not using this word "psychic" as it is usually understood, nor in its every day connotation. The psyche is, literally, the soul within, or the higher self, who emerges from out of the threefold lower self, as the butterfly emerges out of the chrysalis; it is that beautiful reality, which we are going to produce as the result of our life, or lives, down here. The true psychic powers are those which put us in contact with the group. The powers of the physical body, which we use every day, put us in contact with individuals, but when we have developed the powers of the soul, and have unfolded its potentialities, we shall be true psychics. Now what are those powers? All I can do tonight is to enumerate a few out of the many.

One is the conscious control of matter. The majority of us control our physical bodies consciously, making them carry out our behests upon the physical plane. Some of us control our emotions consciously, but very few of us can control the mind. Most of us are controlled by our desires, and by our thoughts. But the time is coming when we shall consciously control our threefold lower nature. Time will then not exist for us at all. We shall have that continuity of consciousness upon the three planes of being—physical, emotional, and mental—which will enable us to live as does the Logos, in that very metaphysical abstraction, the Eternal Now.

Another power of the soul is psychometry. Now what is psychometry? It might be defined as the ability to take a tangible something, belonging perhaps to an individual, and through the medium of that, to put oneself en rapport with that individual, or with a group of individuals. Psychometry is the law of association of ideas applied to the vibratory quality of force for the purpose of obtaining information.

Again, the race will become clairaudient and clairvoyant, which means the capacity to hear and see as clearly and accurately upon the subtler planes as we do upon the physical. It will involve the ability to hear and see all that concerns the group, that is, to hear and see in the fourth and fifth dimensions. I am not enough of a mathematician to attempt to explain these dimensions, and am apt myself to get very confused when considering them, but an illustration that was given me may make the whole thing somewhat clearer. A young Swedish thinker explained it to me thus:

"The fourth dimension is the ability to see through and around a thing. The fifth dimension is the ability, for instance, to take an eye, and by means of that eye to put oneself en rapport with all other eyes in the solar system. To see in the sixth dimension might be defined as the power to take a pebble off the beach, and by means of it to put oneself in accord with the entire planet. Now in the fifth dimension, where you took the eye, you were limited to a particular line of manifestation, but in the case of the sixth dimension, where you took a pebble, you were put in touch with the entire planet." This is something very far ahead of us, but it is interesting to speak about, and holds a promise for each and all.

There is not time to deal with the other powers, nor can I enumerate what they all may be. Healing by touch will be amongst them. The manipulation of the magnetic fluids, and conscious creation by means of colour and sound, are others. All that really concerns us at this time is that we should consciously take ourselves in hand, seek to come ever more and more under the control of the inner ruler, endeavour to become radio-active, and to develop group consciousness.

LECTURE VII.

COSMIC EVOLUTION.

It might well be considered ridiculous for anyone to undertake to give a lecture on Cosmic Evolution, because, of course, it is a subject which neither I nor any other mortal knows anything about, and consequently we are utterly unable to express ourselves upon it. Nevertheless, there are certain deductions we can make under the law of analogy which may lead us to very interesting realms of thought. We have for several weeks been considering the evolution of the atom from stage to stage, until we included the entire solar system under the term "atom".

We studied first, along general lines, the atom of substance, then we studied the human atom, and later we applied what we knew about both these atoms to the still larger sphere, or atom, a planet, which we called a planetary atom; then we extended the idea still further to the atom of the solar system, predicating it as having a position within a still greater whole.

We studied three methods of evolution, or development, in connection with this subject. We considered the aspects which were evolved by means of these atoms, their qualities, or psychic nature, and we saw how in the atom of substance the only psychic quality we could postulate about it was the quality of intelligence. We passed on them to atomic forms, subhuman forms, and saw how the forms in the two kingdoms of nature, the vegetable and animal, demonstrated another quality of the Deity, that of sensation, feeling, or embryo love and emotion; we found that in the animal kingdom also a third quality, that of rudimentary mind, began to show itself, and that when we arrived at the human atom, we had three aspects demonstrating, intelligence, love, and a central will. We extended this concept to the planet and to the solar system, and found that, working out through the form of the solar system, we had a great Intelligence or Mind; that the object of His utilisation of form was the demonstration of another quality, love or wisdom, the whole being energised by a great central WILL. We deduced therefrom that this central Will might be the manifestation of an Entity Who informs the entire system, from the very lowest atom of substance up to that great Life Who energises the planetary scheme.

Having laid down these fundamentals we passed on to the consideration of the evolution of the conscious life within the atomic form, finding that a higher type of consciousness is consistently evolved by each atom; that the human consciousness is distinguished from all other lower forms in that it is self-conscious; that man is an intelligent will, consciously performing every action, becoming aware of his surroundings, and working out a definite line of activity with a specific objective in view. The self-consciousness of man leads on again to something wider still, to the consciousness of the great planetary Spirit, which may perhaps be best expressed in the term 'group consciousness'. As evolution proceeds man will pass from the stage of self-consciousness in which you and I now are, to a realisation of what is meant by group consciousness, something as yet practically unknown, except as some beautiful ideal, and a dream which may, at some distant time, materialise. Group consciousness, again, will logically lead on to that which we, for lack of a better term, might call God-consciousness, though I deprecate the use of the word God because of the many quarrels it causes in the world between the different thinkers of the human family. These differences are founded largely upon differences in phraseology, upon the terms used to express fundamental ideas, and upon varying methods of organisation. When the scientist, for instance, speaks of force, or energy, and the Christian speaks of God, and the Hindu uses terms analogous to the 'I am that I am', or the Self, they are all speaking of one and the same great life, but have lost much time in endeavouring to prove each other wrong, and to demonstrate the accuracy of their own interpretation.

We next saw that, roughly speaking, atomic evolution could be divided into two parts or stages; one stage we called the atomic stage, and another we called, for lack of a better term, the radio-active stage. The atomic stage is that in which the atom pursues its own self-centred life, is concerned entirely with its own evolution, and the effect of the contacts it makes. As evolution proceeds, it becomes apparent that in time the atom begins to react to a greater life outside itself, and in this you have the period analogous to that of the form-building stage, in which these atoms of substance are attracted by a greater charge of energy, or positive electrical force, (if you like to call it such) which draws them, or attracts them to itself, and builds out of them a form; these atoms of substance, in turn, become then electrons. We found, then, how, in your case and mine, as in the case of every self-conscious unit, the same procedure is followed, and that you have a central life holding within the sphere of its influence the atoms that constitute the different bodies, mental, emotional, and physical; that we manifest, that we move and carry on our life, and work out our purposes, by attracting to ourselves the atoms of substance that are adequate to our needs, and through which we can make the necessary contacts. These atoms are to us, the central life, what the electrons are to the central positive charge in the atom of substance. Then we saw that if this is true, namely, that there is a self-centred stage, or purely atomic period, for the atom, and for the human atom, then again for the atom of the planet, indwelt by its central spiritual life, we should be able to predicate logically a similar state of affairs. Thus we were led into the field of speculation. We considered then whether all that transpires upon our planet may not be due to the self-centred condition of the Entity Who is working out His purposes by means of it. Finally we carried forward the same idea in connection with the solar system itself.

We passed on then to the consideration of the second stage, that which the scientist has been studying in connection with the atom of the chemist and physicist for the last twenty years, the radio-active stage; we saw how there was a condition analogous to this in the evolution of the human atom, and that there is a period preceding it which parallels the atomic stage, wherein man is purely selfish, entirely self-centred, and pays no attention to the welfare of the group of which he is a part. This prior stage is very apparent in the world today. A large percentage of the human family is in the atomic stage, but we must remember that it is a protective and necessary one; it is passed through by every unit of the human family in the process of finding its place within the group, and enables it to develop something of value to give to that group when the second stage is entered.

In the world today there are also units of the human family who are passing into the second stage, they are becoming radio-active and magnetic, they influence other forms and are becoming group conscious; they are passing out of the "I am" stage into the "I am that" realisation; the life and purpose of the great Entity of Whose body they are a part, is beginning to be cognised by them; they are becoming aware of the purpose back of the life of the planetary Spirit Who is the subjective impulse lying behind objective manifestation upon our earth. They are beginning to co-operate with His plans, to work for the betterment of their group; and the difference between them and other atoms of the human family is that they are now group conscious, they have a wider horizon, a group recognition, and a larger purpose. At the same time they do not lose their self-consciousness, nor their own individual identity, and their own spheroidal life remains, but they put the whole force and energy which flows through them not into the working out of their own plans, but into an intelligent co-operation with the greater Life of which they are a part. Such men are few and far between, but when they are more in number, then we can look for a change in world conditions, and for that time to arrive, of which St. Paul speaks when he says: "There should be no division in the body, but the members should have the same care one for another. Whether one member suffer, all members suffer with it, or one member be honoured, all rejoice with it.... it is the same God which worketh all in all. There are diversities of gifts but the same spirit; there are differences of ministries (or service) but the same Lord." When we are all group conscious, when we are all aware of the purpose which lies back of manifestation upon our planet, when we are consciously active, and throwing all our energy into the working out of group plans, then we shall have what the Christian calls the "millennium".

Now, if you have in the evolution of the atom of substance, and the human atom, these two stages, if they are the basis of all future development, then within the planetary atom you will have the same two stages, that in which the planetary Life is working out His own plans, and a later one in which He falls in with the greater plans of the Life which animates the solar system. Not yet being in a position to have an interview with the planetary Spirit, I am unable to tell you whether He is as yet co-operating in the purposes of the solar Logos; but we might be able to get some idea of the general purpose by the study of race evolution and the development of the great international plans within the planet. We must bear in mind also, that, though we human beings consider ourselves as the highest and greatest manifestation upon the planet, there may be other evolutions through which the central Life may be working, of which we know as yet but little. We must study not only man, but should consider also the angel evolution, or the deva evolution, as the Hindu calls it. This opens up for us an immense field of study and speculation.

Again, within the solar system we shall expect to find analogous stages. We shall find, probably, that the great Life animating the entire solar system, the great Entity Who is using it for the working out of a definite purpose, energises it by means of these great centres of force which we call planetary atoms; that these centres, in their turn, work by means of lesser centres or groups, passing their energy on down through groups of human atoms to the various kingdoms of nature, and thus to the little atom of substance which, in its turn, reflects the entire solar system. This question of atomic life, if we think it out, is vastly interesting, and leads us into many lines of conjecture. One of the main points of interest which it opens up is the intimate correlation, and close interaction of the atoms of every kind, and the all-pervading unity which must ultimately be recognised. If we have found that there comes a stage in the evolution of all atoms of every kind in which they feel and search for their place within the group, and from being positive become negative in regard to a greater life, if it is true in all these manifestations of consciousness there is a self-conscious stage and a group conscious stage, is it not logical and possible that perhaps, after all, our solar system is but an atom within a greater whole? May there not be for our solar system, and our solar Logos, a central larger life towards which the informing Spirit within the solar sphere is gradually attracted, and towards Whose consciousness our Deity aspires? Are there anywhere indications of such an attractive force, or goal? Are there greater spheres of solar life outside our system, that have a definite effect upon it? This may be but a speculation, but it has its points of interest. If we study astronomical books, and seek to ascertain whether astronomers say that this is so, we shall meet with a vast amount of contradictory opinion; we shall find that some astronomers say that within the Pleiades is a central point around which our solar system revolves; others say that in the constellation of Hercules, is the point of magnetic attraction for our solar system. On the other hand, you will find this flatly contradicted. We shall find some astronomers talking about "star-drift," and saying that the drift, or trend, of certain stars is in a specific direction; others argue that the distances are so vast that it is impossible to determine whether certain systems are following a definite orbit or not.

Nevertheless, if we go to some of the ancient books, those which we call mythological (and a myth may be defined as something which holds a great truth hidden until we are ready to understand it), and if we study the ancient books of the East, we shall find that in all of them there are two or three constellations which are regarded as having a peculiarly intimate relation to our solar system. Towards these views modern astronomers as yet hold an agnostic attitude, and from the point of view of materialistic science, rightly so. What I seek to emphasize here is that a topic upon which scientists and astronomers are divided, yet which is nevertheless a subject of contention, and one upon which the oriental books sound a clear note, must have a basis in fact, and that there is probably an aspect of truth in the assertion. I would personally suggest here that that aspect of truth will be found, not along *physical* lines of interpretation, but along the lines of *consciousness;* that it is the psychic evolution that is going on within all atoms (using psychic in the sense of the subjective consciousness) which is hinted at in these books, and the emphasis is laid upon our having an occult relationship with other solar systems. Here the truth may perhaps be found. The life subjective may be one; the energy flowing between them may be one; but in the physical form lies diversity. Perhaps in the evolution of the intelligence, in the manifestation of love, or group consciousness, and in the development of will or purpose, lies unity, the one-ness of the subjective life, and the eventual recognition that within the form, and in the form only, lies separation and differentiation.

The ancient books of the East point out, in considering this subject, that the seven stars of the Great Bear, the seven stars of the Pleiades, and the sun Sirius, have a very close connection with our solar system, and that they hold an intimate psychic magnetic relation to our solar Logos. We have seen that the goal for the atom of substance is self-consciousness; and that for the Entity Who is evolving through a planet, the goal may be God consciousness. Now, of course, when you consider the solar Logos words fail, yet for Him also there must be a goal. You can call this Absolute Consciousness, if you like. Let us again illustrate this. Our body, we have been told, is made up of a multiplicity of little lives, or cells, or atoms, each having its own individual consciousness. This corresponds to its self-consciousness. The consciousness of the physical body, viewed as a whole, might, from the atom's point of view, be regarded as its group consciousness. Then we have the consciousness of man, the thinker. He is the one who energises the body, and turns it to his will; that is, to the atom in his body, analogous to what we might call God consciousness. Our self-conscious realisation is as far removed from that of the atom as the consciousness of the solar Logos is from ours. Now to the atom in our body that consciousness of the solar Logos might be called Absolute Consciousness, might it not? This thought can be extended to the human atom, to the planetary atom, and you can further predicate that the solar Logos reaches out to a consciousness beyond His own analogous to that which stretches between the atom in your body and Him. Here you have a very marvellous vista opening up. Yet this is, in itself, encouraging; for if we study closely the cell in a physical body, and consider the long road that has been travelled between its consciousness, and that which a man now knows to be his, we have for ourselves the promise and hope of future achievement, and the incentive to persist in our endeavour.

The old books of the East have held secreted for many ages the truth about much which is only now beginning to sink into the consciousness of the occidental. They taught the radio-activity of matter thousands of years ago, and so perhaps, after all, there may be an equal amount of truth in their teaching about the constellations. Perhaps in the stars that we can see in the distant heavens, and in the life that is evolving within them, we have the objective of our solar Logos, and the influences that are flowing towards him, attracting him towards them, and making him, in due course of time, radio-active. In the Eastern books they say that in the sun Sirius lies the source of wisdom, and that the influence or the energy of love emanates from there. Then they say that there is a constellation that is even more closely connected with our solar Logos, the reason being that He is not, as yet, sufficiently evolved so that He can respond completely to Sirius, but He can respond to the influence of the seven sisters or the Pleiades. This group is a most interesting one. If you will go to the dictionary and look up the word "electricity", you will find it suggested that it may be traced back to the star Electra, one of the seven sisters, and supposed by some to be the little lost Pleiad. The Eastern teachers say that in the mystery of electricity is hidden all knowledge, and that when we have fathomed that we shall know all there is to be known. What the relationship of the Pleiades to our solar system may be, it is not possible for us to say, but even our Christian Bible recognises it, and Job speaks of "the sweet influences of the Pleiades," whilst some of the Oriental Scriptures affirm that the connection lies in sound, or vibration. Perhaps the Pleiades are the source of the atomic life of our Logos, the active intelligent aspect, that one which was first developed, and which we might call electrical matter.

Then there is the Great Bear. There is much that is interesting said about the relation between the Great Bear and the Pleiades in Oriental writings. The seven sisters are said to be the seven wives of the seven stars of the Great Bear. Now what is perhaps the truth back of that legend? If the Pleiades are the source of electrical manifestation, the active intelligent aspect of the solar system, and their energy that which animates all matter, they may perhaps represent the negative aspect, whose polar opposite, or the positive aspect, is their seven husbands, the seven stars of the Great Bear. Perhaps the union of these two is what produces our solar system. Perhaps these two types of energy, one from the Pleiades, and the other from the Great Bear, meet, and in their conjunction produce that blazing forth in the heavens which we call our solar system.

The relationship of these two constellations, or rather their subjective relationship, must surely have some basis in fact, or we would not have it hinted at in the different mythologies. There must be something that connects them, out of all the myriads of constellations, with our solar system. But when we endeavour to give it a purely physical application we go astray. If we work it out along the lines of the subjective life, and connect it with energy, quality, or force, we are liable to stumble upon truth, and find out some of the reality which may underly what appears at first sight to be a senseless fable. Anything that widens our horizon, that enables us to take a broader vision and a clearer view of what is going on in the evolutionary process, is of value to us, not because the accumulation of ascertained facts is of value, but because of what it enables us to do within ourselves; our ability to think in wider and larger terms is increased; we are enabled to look beyond our self-centred point of view, and to include within our consciousness other and different aspects than our own. In doing this we are developing group consciousness, and we shall realise eventually that the apparently stupendous facts which we fought and died for down the ages, and emphasised as the entire truth, were after all but fragments of a plan, and infinitesimal portions of a gigantic sum total. Perhaps, therefore, when we come back to earth again, and can look back upon the things that interest us now, and which we consider so important, we shall find how erroneous facts were as we then apprehended them. Facts, after all, do not matter; the facts of the last century are not facts now, and in the next century scientists may laugh at our dogmatic assertions, and wonder how we could have looked upon matter as we did. It is the development of the life, and the relationship of the life to all that is around, that really matters; and, above all, the effect that we are having upon those with whom we are associated, and the work we do, which affects, for better or for worse, the group in which we find ourselves.

In closing this series of lectures, I cannot do better than quote again from St. Paul, where he says: "I reckon that the sufferings of this present time are not worthy to be compared with the glory which shall be revealed in us ......for we are saved by hope......for I am persuaded that neither death nor life, nor angels nor principalities, nor powers, nor things present, nor things to come, nor height, nor depth, nor any other creature, shall be able to separate us from the love of God."

FINIS